No Room to Move

The bizarre world of the Watchtower Society

Alan Butters

ST IVES MEDIA

ISBN: 978-0-9922675-4-4

Contents

Contents iii

Author's note 7

Introduction 10

Where It Began 12

Why Does It Work? 21

Let Thy Kingdom Come 45

An Excusive Club 75

The Trouble With Science 105

A Question of Inerrancy 136

Separate From the World 148

When Things Go Wrong 168

A Dangerous Perspective 184

The Heart of The Matter 202

Conclusion 213

Afterward 215

References 221

Glossary of Watchtower Society Terms 237

Index 251

For Nicole, who saved me.

.

Author's note

I wrote *No Room to Move* in 1994 after disassociating myself from the Watchtower Society; a decision that was a long time coming but inevitable nevertheless. The title pretty much summed up how I had been feeling for some time. In addition to being a sort of diary-therapy, the book had a purpose. My plan was to have three copies bound and to give a copy to each of my children when they were old enough to appreciate another perspective on a religion into which, like me, they had been raised.

My plan quickly began to unravel after I gave the first of the books to my oldest son when he turned 18. Unsurprisingly, the elders from the local congregation took a dim view of the whole endeavor and were immediately mobilized to protect their flock, including my own children who were considered to be "fatherless boys" since my departure from the Jehovah's witnesses.

Having no control over me, pressure was brought to

bear on my family. My parents were essentially told that to continue seeing me and allowing me to visit their home would affect their own standing within the congregation. They were strongly encouraged to only have contact with me that was unavoidable and certainly not ever to allow me into their home. While my mother was reluctantly willing to comply with the controls being forced upon them, my father to his everlasting credit was not. He was stripped of the small duties (known as privileges by Jehovah's Witnesses) that he performed within his congregation as a measure of his previous standing. A small thing to most outsiders but a reprimand and loss of face for him and my mother no less.

His resolve meant that I could continue to see my parents occasionally which at the time was no small thing considering that every other person that I knew within the Jehovah's witness community was now shunning me because of my decision to leave the organisation. Out of respect for his decision and not wanting to fuel the fire any further, I decided that my book project should be mothballed for as long as he was alive.

Following my father's sudden death in June 2013, I felt that the time had come to bring to a wider audience a glimpse into the bizarre world of the Watchtower Society. What follows then is largely the book I wrote in 1994 with minor changes to aid readability. Despite these changes, the reader is warned that many of the doctrines discussed are complex and the "logic" behind them is challenging to explain. Patience and perseverance will be required, particular in the area of the establishment of pivotal

Watchtower Society dates such as 1914.

With the benefit of almost twenty years of hindsight my perspective has obviously shifted since I first wrote the book and I'll have more to say about that in the Afterward following the original text.

Alan Butters, July 2013

Introduction

I guess that I knew I had to do something when the local Doctor sat on the edge of my hospital bed and said "Alan, before you leave this place I want to know exactly what plans you're making to sort out your life."

That was in November 1992 and was without a doubt the lowest point in my life.

My real problem was that I didn't want to be a Jehovah's Witness. On the surface this might not seem like a decision that merits a meltdown, but that would be to underestimate the power the movement has over its adherents.

In this story I will strive to explain why I came to that decision, why it was such a difficult one and why leaving the movement almost cost me my sanity. I will also trace the history of the organisation and outline its operation, structure and methods as well as discussing the beliefs and doctrines that so totally guide the lives of millions of people around the globe.

I will attempt to show how the organisation and not the Bible is seen as the ultimate authority by the Witnesses, how the organisation wields power over individual members and legislates in areas that ought properly to be the domain of conscience. I will demonstrate how, in the Witness theology, the Bible is not allowed to speak for itself. I will also discuss the chequered history of the organisation and its founders in the area of prophecy and its presumptuous claim to be the only channel of true spiritual direction on earth.

I will outline my own difficulties in grappling with the fundamentalist view of the Bible as a work of absolute inerrancy and the mental struggle that it caused me. In the disparate areas of science and Bible translation I will demonstrate what in my estimation is the intellectual dishonesty of the Watchtower Society.

I am not a Bible scholar, nor do I have any formal theological training. What I bring to this account is simply a fascination with the Bible as literature, an inquiring mind and a conviction that the human spirit should not be crushed by nonsensical dogma.

My reasons for writing about this experience are my own and are not intended as a personal attack on any individual member of the Jehovah's Witness organisation. Indeed, I have counted many of them as friends over the years. The organisation to which they belong however is a different matter, and about it I have some grave misgivings.

Alan Butters, August 1994

Where It Began

"Nor deem the irrevocable past as
wholly wasted, wholly vain, if rising
on its wrecks, at least to something
nobler we attain."

Henry Wadsworth Longfellow

To put the story into some context, a few words
are in order regarding my own beginnings.

I was born on the 24th of July 1956 in Yorkshire,
England. In 1965 my parents, myself and a two year
old brother emigrated to Australia and settled in the
eastern suburbs of Melbourne.

It was in 1967 and my eleventh year that we
received a knock on the door that would change our
lives forever, shattering my father's large family and
pushing my brother and me to our emotional and

mental limits.

The door knocker was a middle aged man with a message of hope and salvation that caused my father to feel that he had found something akin to a hidden treasure, an experience not uncommon in the New Testament narrative.

The middle aged man was of course a Jehovah's Witness, and like most Witnesses, was skilled in the use of the Bible and other literature and had been well trained in the art of making converts. He was in fact the product of an intensive ministry training program that examined every likely argument and objection that my father could have raised. He also had an arsenal of literature provided by an organisation that measures the publication of its fortnightly journals by the tens of millions[1]. My father was convinced that he had found the truth at last and forged ahead with all the classic fervour of the religious zealot.

Initially, my mother wanted nothing of this new religion and threatened to leave my father if he persisted. He had already been forewarned to expect opposition to his new course and so considered this to be proof positive that he was doing the right thing. Realising that he could not be dissuaded, my mother eventually joined him, although never matching his pace, and my brother and I were raised from then on in the light of Watchtower teaching.

Anxious to please and to be accepted by my peers I was baptised as a Witness at the age of sixteen and apart from a lapse in my early twenties of two years continued to make progress in the organisation until the age of twenty six when I was appointed as a

Ministerial Servant with responsibility for managing the accounts of the local congregation. At the age of thirty three I was appointed to serve as an Elder in the congregation. I will discuss this position later when outlining the organisation's structure, but suffice to say that it is a position of considerable responsibility and is the goal held out to all Witness men but achieved by only a minority.

It was from this position that I began to seriously question the validity of what I had been taught and had indeed taught many others. The uncertainties and doubts that had plagued me for many years now took on a higher profile as greater loyalty to the organisation was expected. My world was beginning to crumble from within.

----oooo----

Before continuing, let me trace the history of the organisation and outline its structure and the methods that make it one of the fastest growing religions in the world today.

The modern day organisation that is Jehovah's Witnesses had its Genesis in Pittsburgh Pennsylvania when Charles Taze Russell rejected the teachings of the Congregational Church in which he had been raised and established a Bible study group of his own in the year 1870 at the tender age of eighteen[2]. Russell approached the Scriptures with the notion that their interpretation must be subject to human reason. Using this process, he developed his "Present Truth" theology, which was characterised by a rejection of virtually every major Christian doctrine as "unreasonable and unscriptural" and was punctuated by a strong aversion to organised religion and government.[3]

In 1879 he began publishing the magazine which is today distributed globally as the *Watchtower*.[4] Russell denounced the teaching of Christian denominations because of the conflict he saw between the notion of a loving God and the idea of eternal torment.[5] Despite having much scandal attached to his name, Russell had a loyal following that considered him (as he considered himself) to be God's chosen instrument for communication.[6] Upon Russell's death in 1916 he was replaced by Joseph (Judge) Rutherford who published many books and tracts, directing the work of the organisation from Brooklyn New York[7]. Unlike his predecessor, Rutherford had some formal training and was a practising lawyer (although there is a question as to whether he actually received a law degree). The sobriquet of Judge seems to have been well chosen by Rutherford as, following in Russell's footsteps he too decided what the followers ought to believe.[8]

It was at the annual convention of the Watchtower Society in 1931 that Rutherford announced the name change to Jehovah's Witnesses based on a section of scripture in the book of Isaiah[9].

Rutherford was succeeded in 1942 by Nathan Knorr who in turn was replaced by the former Vice President, Frederick Franz in 1977[10]. Franz had spent two years studying Greek at the University of Cincinnati but was self taught in Hebrew. Despite this, he acted as principle translator in the production of the Witnesses' own Bible translation.[11] It was also in the seventies that real control was transferred to a small council of about a dozen men known as the Governing Body in an attempt to bring the organisation in line with what was perceived to be first century practice[12].

Until this turbulent time the existing governing body had been little more than a rubber stamp committee for the all powerful president. The change meant that the governing body held the same dictatorial power that the presidents Russell and Rutherford once wielded over the flock. Members of this governing body are not elected, replacement members are selected by the current body.

Three corporations direct the activities of Jehovah's Witnesses; the Watchtower Bible and Tract Society of Pennsylvania, the Watchtower Bible and Tract Society, Inc. of New York, and the International Bible Students Association.[13]

The organisation has extensive printing facilities around the world, all staffed by thousands of volunteers who work largely for food and board with literature being distributed internationally by door knocking campaigns on a non profit basis. By the late 1980s the Witnesses had published ten billion pieces of literature.[14]

The Witnesses strive to be self sufficient in their printing operations building their own factories and worker's accommodation, and having extensive farming operations to provide food for those employed in the factories. The printing equipment is maintained wherever possible by witnesses. All of the cooking, cleaning and washing is done by witness staff and even the transport of literature is by their own fleet of trucks and drivers. The Witnesses have also made use of the latest computer technology and developed a number of their own systems for multi language translation. The only real contact that many of these workers have with the world outside is when they engage in their weekly preaching work.

The activities of the organisation are funded from donations and the sale of literature and operates as a non profit society.[15]

Much of the prodigious output from the organisation's numerous printing facilities is funnelled into training programs for its members. Jehovah's Witnesses are expected to attend and participate in five meetings per week, most of which are designed to promote the skills and attitudes needed to optimise the door to door preaching work. Members are trained in the use of the Bible, in reasoning, and in leading the minds of others to accept their interpretation of the scriptures.

A regular meeting is set aside each week as a public speaking school with all members expected to participate, including children from the time they can read. In addition to this the *Watchtower* magazine is used at one weekly meeting as a study basis while another meeting is held for smaller groups in private homes. There is even a weekly meeting that concentrates specifically on the methods and tactics that can be employed to counter opposition and overcome the protestations of disinterested and often disgruntled householders.[16]

As could be expected, this study program produces Ministers well versed in Watchtower theology with minds focused on the task of preaching to others at every opportunity. This zeal has taken their work to over two hundred lands and islands of the globe.[17] All Witnesses are expected to share in this work including children. I estimate that I have spent in excess of five thousand hours preaching door to door.

The work is directed from Brooklyn in New York via headquarters in many countries and down through a chain of overseers presiding over progressively smaller geographical areas. The direct link to the flock is through a body of elders[18] in each congregation. This body (men only) is charged with the welfare of all in the congregation.

These men can be called on to provide counsel in almost all areas of life and in delivering this they will use the Bible and the myriad of Watchtower publications at their disposal. Indeed it is hard to imagine an area of life that is not covered by a Witness publication. This includes even what most individuals would consider private affairs such as dress, grooming, employment, associations, music, literature, cinema, television, dancing, morals, holidays, food, drink, education, hobbies, medical treatment and so on.[19] The results from this level of proscription will be discussed later.

The activity of each individual Witness in the preaching work is also monitored closely with everyone expected to hand in an itemised report at the end of each month.[20] Much is placed on this report, and indeed it is not possible to progress through the organisation unless this report demonstrates a zeal and commitment toward the preaching activity. Members are expected to indicate on their reports the number of hours actually spent in the door to door work, the number of books and magazines sold to householders, the number of return visits made on interested parties, the number of *Watchtower* magazine subscriptions sold and the number of individuals with whom the Witness conducts Bible study lessons. The national averages in each country are held up as targets for minimum levels of activity.

It has been observed by a former member of the governing body of Jehovah's Witnesses that the figures from these reports worldwide are "studied with the same avid interest that a large corporation would study the figures of its production records, its business growth."[21]

There are also special Ministers that agree to devote larger numbers of hours in the preaching work on a full time basis. One such capacity is that of "Pioneer"[22] where the individual Witness strives for ninety to one hundred and forty hours in the preaching work each month and for which concessions on literature costs are given. I engaged in this work for two years before marrying in the mid seventies. The Pioneers are expected to take the lead in the preaching work and to assist newer or more timid ones to become proficient.

All of this emphasis on recruitment ensures that the faithful stay focused on the disciple making work and as a result the numbers continue to grow. Jehovah's Witnesses are in fact recognised for this work and most people will have had the experience of a door step sermon. Between 1986 and 1992 the Witnesses spent 2,715,998,934 hours engaged in the preaching work.[23]

In addition to their door to door work, they are also industrious builders with a program of ongoing "quick builds".[24] This involves the building of local meeting places or Kingdom Halls as they are known, in just three days. So organised are they that from a concrete slab on day one, a totally finished, painted, carpeted, landscaped hall emerges by the afternoon of day three including heating and sound system, with seating for two hundred and fifty people in upholstered seats. Teams of approximately one thousand workers accomplish this feat at the rate of one hall per month. Their organisational skills and dedication to the task at hand cannot be faulted.

The picture begins to emerge of a society within society that has its own rules and regulations, not divided by race or colour, able to accomplish vast amounts of work, highly organised and directed, with a great sense of loyalty within and to the organisation.

The how and why of this phenomenon will be examined in the next section.

The cost in terms of the human spirit and free thinking will be explored later.

Why Does It Work?

"O! it is excellent
To have a giant's strength, but it is tyrannous
To use it like a giant."

Isabella, *Measure for Measure*, William Shakespeare.

Why are people attracted to this organisation in the first place? What motivates them to persevere in the difficult activity of knocking on their neighbour's door when they know in most cases that they are unwelcome? Why do they live a life of separateness from the community while at the same time existing as a part of it? Why do they allow an organisation to tell them what to read and what not to read, how to think and what to believe?

I suppose the answers to these questions will vary from individual to individual, but my experience suggests that some common threads can be identified and in this chapter I will attempt to list these factors.

Protection from the world

Imagine a small child at a circus. The traditional lion tamer is in the ring and with his whip and chair makes the mighty animals do his bidding. Around the ring is a steel fence approximately ten feet high that keeps the animals in and the humans out. But consider, is the fence a protection or a restriction? In the mind of the child the fence may be a restriction to a better view, whereas most adults would see it as an essential protection. This may hold true in many areas of life, where what appears to one person as a restriction appeals to another as a protection.

This illustrates the Witnesses' reasoning concerning restrictions on thought and action imposed by the Watchtower Society. In fact to them they are not restrictions at all but serve in their own estimation as a protection from the badness of the world. And lest anyone doubt that protection is required, Witnesses are encouraged to look at the world and its problems as here, all are told, is proof positive that ignoring the Watchtower Society's guidelines results in murder, hatred, venereal disease and drug abuse. The literature of the organisation is used to highlight every problem mankind faces, every failing of science, politics and religion together with rising crime rates.[1]

Once this protection-not-restriction frame of mind

is embraced, every atrocity reported in the news, every child that is molested, every woman that is raped strengthens what to the Witnesses is irrefutable proof that they are on the right track as all of these atrocities are committed by individuals who have no regard for the law of God. The logic is, of course, that anyone who loves God would not do such things.

Let us examine this reasoning. We are all accustomed to living our lives with some sort of limits or restrictions. For example, when we travel in our vehicles most of us fasten our seat belts even though we could be more comfortable without them. We stop at a red light even when we might be in a hurry. Why do we do this? Because of the fact that to do so is a protection for us. So it cannot be denied that some things that appear to restrict us exist in fact for our own interests. A reasonable person is able to see the benefits served by these devices in the broader sense even though they may prove irritating under some circumstances.

But imagine for a moment that the government of the day proposes to legislate that in addition to wearing our seat belt while driving, we must also have a full racing harness fitted, must don a fire proof suit and wear a crash helmet. An argument could be mounted that this is for our own good. After all, professional racing car drivers wear this equipment for safety so why not everyone? I suspect that most people would consider this an outrageous restriction of their freedom. Why? Is it because we don't believe we would be safer wearing this equipment? No, most reasonable people would acknowledge that if involved in a serious accident their chance of survival would be greater when wearing such protection.

The point is that we would see the wearing of so much equipment as excessive. It would make the routines of daily life very difficult and uncomfortable. So we are prepared to tolerate a certain level of increased risk because we recognise that we have to live and function in the real world. This principle holds true in many areas of our lives.

Take a construction worker on a building site. His work presents him with many dangers. Does this mean he will work in a suit of armour? Of course not. The worker recognises that to be totally insulated from danger would render him unable to do his work.

So it goes with the Witnesses who accept a level of restriction far in excess of what most people would consider reasonable. Allowing their lives to be directed to the extent of being told what is and is not appropriate to think, leaves them unable to function effectively in the real world. As we will see, it develops in many a suspicion of authority, an inability to think critically, an unwillingness to shoulder personal responsibility and to plan for the future, a dismissive attitude to the value of education and an intolerance towards the beliefs of others.

Witnesses must create their own society and then operate within its walls in order to cope. It suggests that all the difficulties of humankind can be simplified down to one choice, namely, to be a Witness and be protected or not to be a witness and be in danger. What this view fails to take into account of course is the fact that millions of other fundamental Christian groups that live by a strict moral code are also protected from many evils to the same extent as are Witnesses.

But more to the point, millions of other humans that are not religious in any way or who subscribe to non Christian beliefs are also protected in the same manner simply by the way they choose to live their lives. They may elect not to be promiscuous or choose to engage in safe sex practices. They may resolve not to use addictive drugs and may by deliberate thought have respect for their neighbour. These people can live happy productive and meaningful lives without ever setting foot inside a church.

At this point one may wonder why most Witnesses don't see this seemingly self evident fact of life. The reason is fairly simple. They do not associate with people who are not Jehovah's Witnesses. The *Watchtower* magazine leaves no doubt as to who are acceptable associations for its members as the following definition shows:

"Approved association with Jehovah's Witnesses requires accepting the entire range of the true teachings of the Bible, including those Scriptural beliefs that are unique to Jehovah's Witnesses."[2] Accordingly, the Witnesses although compelled to rub shoulders with "worldly" people at work or school, do not develop friendships or spend time socially with such ones.

A parallel may be drawn with the use of propaganda during times of war. It was none other than Adolf Hitler who said:

"As soon as by one's own propaganda even a

glimpse of right on the other side is admitted, the cause for doubting one's own right is laid."[3]

Likewise with the Witnesses. The us-and-them attitude is maintained by not allowing oneself to get close to non Witnesses and thus realise that in essence such persons are no different, having the same hopes and fears for their children, sharing in the same joys and pains of life, and trying to live their lives as peacefully as possible.

This in fact has been the major trouble in my mind during the time I have been associated with Jehovah's Witnesses. It seems to me that the unity they achieve is at the expense of their attitude to the rest of humanity. The fact that others are essentially no different to them seems to be overshadowed by their artificial separation of the world into Witness and non Witness.

A New World Society

A basic doctrine of the Witnesses that will be explored later is their belief that God will purge the earth of all who are not Witnesses or favourably disposed toward them. This will allow those left to be the foundation of a new world society, although I suspect this was not what George Bush had in mind when he used the term. This new society will enjoy endless life in a paradise earth where no crime, sickness, death or badness of any kind (including, one presumes, no contrary opinion) will exist.[4] This prospect for an end to badness attracts many people to the organisation.

Let us explore the implications of that belief for a moment. There are about eight million Jehovah's witnesses earth wide. If we are generous and allow another twelve million to be righteously disposed sympathisers then that brings us to a nice even figure of twenty million persons. If we round off the earth's population to seven billion, a simple calculation reveals that approximately 0.3% of the earth's inhabitants would survive the destruction that the Witnesses promise. Visualise the Melbourne Cricket Ground packed with one hundred thousand excited people and then picture a dreadful earthquake or some other natural disaster leaving only 0.3% of that number surviving. It translates to three hundred survivors if we employ the same rate of survival postulated by the Witnesses for the end of the world. Three hundred survivors from a crowd of one hundred thousand. The God of the Witnesses appears to be exceptionally choosy.

We will explore later why the Witnesses hold to this doctrine and the effect that it has upon their thinking, but it should be obvious that such a view serves to divide Witnesses from non Witnesses. After all, why become close to someone who has no future? So the organisation is drawn together strongly and its members see themselves as only temporary residents within society.[5]

The appealing things that flow from this exclusive philosophy include comradeship, a sense of belonging, a feeling of privilege or superiority and a hope for the future. We will deal later with the price that is exacted for these comforts.

An uncomplicated world view

Many people today are distressed to see the state to which the world has descended. They despair when the media shows footage of the famines and violence that seem to be an integral part of society today. Some feel powerless to help or to change things and cannot understand why humans treat their neighbours with such disrespect and indifference.

It is for this attitude that Witnesses look.[6] The solution that they present is simple in concept: God will not tolerate this world forever and is determined to sweep away wickedness. Images such as a giant's hand wiping our earthly globe clean leap out from the covers of Watchtower literature. The publications inevitably proceed to outline the steps required for survival. The existence of such a prospect comes as an enormous relief to some. Problems that seemed insurmountable are no longer theirs to solve. They need not be responsible for what happens because someone else (in this case God) will rectify things. This is not to say they no longer care, their tears at the images of starving children are as real as anyone else's, *but they no longer have the responsibility to do anything about it.* This comes as an enormous relief to those who feel powerless or overwhelmed.

What is actually happening here however, is that the Watchtower Society doctrine is simply being used as a way of escaping responsibility. This in itself is a common human tendency. M. Scott Peck in his famous work *The Road Less Travelled* pointed out this fact:

"Whenever we seek to avoid the responsibility for our own behaviour, we do so by attempting to give that responsibility to some other individual or organisation or entity. But this means we then give away our power to that entity, be it "fate" or "society" or the government or the corporation or our boss... In attempting to avoid the pain of responsibility, millions and even billions daily attempt to escape from freedom."[7]

The doctrine of the Watchtower Society provides such an escape. An escape not just from responsibility, but from freedom itself. Freedom to make our own decisions and the responsibility that this brings. Freedom to decide for ourselves and make personal choices in areas about which we feel strongly. As Peck notes, many take the easy way out and submerge themselves in an authority structure which effectively removes this freedom and the frightening responsibility that accompanies it.

As time progresses and the new Witnesses are convinced that their only real responsibility to mankind is to spread the word of the impending destruction from God, they are in fact discouraged from spending time on any other pursuit.[8] It follows from this that all of the efforts man makes to repair the damage he has wrought will be in vain, simply rearranging the deck chairs on the Titanic. In fact to become involved in Greenpeace for example or other conservation societies or perhaps famine relief agencies just takes time from the real work of preaching and, as the world is about to be cleansed, it's pointless anyway.

All of the humanitarian activities to which so many devote their lives are seen in the light of the impending destruction to be pointless distractions. This passive not-my-problem outlook is even smuggled into the Witnesses' own Bible, the *New World Translation* (NWT). In Matthew chapter five and verse nine the NWT has Jesus saying *"Happy are the peaceable."* The literal meaning of the Greek word rendered in the NWT as "peaceable" is "peace-maker" and this is the form used by most Bible translators. Why has the Watchtower Society chosen "peaceable" for this verse? Because their doctrinal position is that Christians should involve themselves in preaching work and wait for peace to be restored to the earth by God rather than being *peace makers* and exerting themselves to ensure this outcome.

Religious organisations such as the Salvation Army are sneered at by many Witnesses who perceive their works to be simply tinkering impotently at the edges of a hopeless situation. After living within the Witness community for twenty five years I can attest to the fact that views similar to these are widely held. This seems to me a most unfortunate outcome within a Christian community.

A framework of values

Another reason why the Witnesses enjoy success (in company with other fundamentalist groups) is that they promote a return to what is seen as the old values. A significant number of people within our society are comfortable with the traditional moral values of the Bible and conclude that Jehovah's Witnesses are practising these. This seems particularly attractive to those individuals disenchanted with mainstream religion and who seek an alternative to what appears to them as religious compromise. The Witnesses are not plagued by issues such as women priests, gay ministers or involvement in politics as these are simply forbidden.

These values are strongly enforced, anyone that behaves in a way that threatens these values is dealt with by the judicial arm of the organisation. This discipline can take many forms from private counselling through to total banishment for those seen to have no remorse over their actions.[9] These actions both protect the value system from erosion and stand as a warning to those thinking of testing it.

Having such a system of values does not of course prevent any individual Witness from falling for any of the world's enticements, but the isolation of the wayward person from the rest of the congregation by judicial action restricts the extent to which those remaining might sympathise. We will discuss this process in chapter eight.

Proof by logic

Although many sorts of people are present within the ranks of the Watchtower organisation, it is clear to me that to a large extent it is self selecting. I agree with the observation of Dr. Walter Martin that:

"The Jehovah's Witness movement appeals chiefly

to a certain type of individual who, lacking a strong feeling of security, finds a definite psychological outlet in an organisation which sets its face against *all* religions and offers a paradise of pleasure to the lonely and the downtrodden of the earth."[10]

Whereas some individuals may be drawn to the history and tradition of the Catholic church for example, and others might be attracted to the family values promoted by the Mormons, Jehovah's Witnesses claim that the true religion can be identified by an application of logic and reasoning.[11] This appeals to those who may have shunned what they perceive to be the sentimentality and ambiguities of other faiths and who feel the need to prove a matter before believing it.

It is worth pausing at this point to consider the nature of proof and logic. When we use the word "proof" it may call to our minds a courtroom scene. Perhaps we have never been in a court but we understand this to be the place where the word "proof" finds a home. We also know that in these hallowed institutions a matter must be proven beyond reasonable doubt.

The familiar process employed to achieve this outcome of course involves two opposing sides, each presenting evidence and a panel of hopefully unbiased onlookers considering where the weight of evidence lies. Of course the system is not perfect and has its detractors, but the concept of weighing the evidence for and against with its basis in logic, if applied fairly, is something with which most people appear comfortable. Indeed, we apply this process often in our daily lives and dealings with others including our own children.

This process, the witnesses pursuade the prospective convert, we will apply to the search for the true religion and prove that we alone have it. I will examine the nature of the proofs themselves in chapter four, but let us dwell here on the manner in which the proof is presented to would-be Jehovah's Witnesses.

It is my observation that the vast majority of those who become Jehovah's Witnesses come from either non religious backgrounds or from mainstream churches where the impact on their lives from the intellectual aspects of any inherited belief system is relatively minimal. It is highly unusual for a new Witness convert to be made from other fundamentalist groups.

The point here is that in most cases the prospective convert has a very limited Bible knowledge when compared to the Witness Minister and so very quickly the teacher / pupil relationship is forged. Jehovah's Witnesses are accustomed to receiving favourable comments from interested persons regarding their skill at finding Bible texts and their ability to answer the householder's many questions.

In our example of a courtroom where matters are proven, there are always two sides when evidence is presented. The concept of the prosecutor presenting evidence for the defence doesn't exist and for obvious reasons. It would hardly result in a fair trial.

Contrast this with the proof offered by the Witnesses. As the quest for truth precedes on the doorstep, who presents the case for the rest of the world's faiths or for science or politics or humanitarianism generally? The Witness of course. And it is no wonder that the rest of the world's cases look a little shaky when compared to the Witnesses.' It is an interesting feature of the Witnesses' publications that arguments running counter to their line of reasoning are selectively presented and then demolished.[12] The Watchtower Society thus acts as both the prosecutor and the defence and so inevitably the outcome is predictable.

Considering this one sided pitch, the prospective convert can be lulled into thinking that she has indeed examined the evidence against the Witnesses' case and found it wanting. The would-be Witness may even believe that they have proven the Watchtower's religious doctrines to be true by this method.

What has happened in fact is that the householder has followed a certain line of reasoning, carefully crafted and practised and has come to the only conclusion possible without recourse to outside information. It should be understood that the Witness, having been convinced by this same method themselves, teaches with all sincerity and fervour.

Why, one might be forgiven for asking, does not the householder simply go to the library and perform her own independent research to verify the Witnesses' case? In fact some do in the early stages, but it proves to be a daunting task. The problem is that the householder often lacks the depth of religious knowledge needed to sort through the many interpretations they will likely come across during the research and the Witnesses argument may seem clear and logical.

Whatever the prospective convert is likely to uncover at this stage can usually be dealt with by the Witness as the householder is likely to be more confused than informed by a research session at the library. Indeed it will probably not be for several years before the new Witness starts questioning her beliefs and by this stage there are many other mechanisms in place to hold her as we will see.

The New World Translation

This section would not be complete without reference to the Witnesses' own translation of the Bible, *The New World Translation of the Holy Scriptures* and the advantage it confers toward the success of their proselytising efforts.

While it is true that the Witnesses allege that the truth from the Bible can be gleaned from any translation, most of their indoctrination is done using the *New World Translation*. Even if a prospective Witness were to begin her studies using an alternative translation it's usually not long before the person is steered toward a view that regards the NWT as the final authority.

Many of the Witnesses' key doctrines are supported by this particular version and it is the one translation used internationally by all Jehovah's Witnesses. This is not to say that an individual Witness is forbidden to look at another translation but it is fair to say that should a question of interpretation arise, the NWT will always be the authority. Indeed, a Witness using another translation as their principle text would be frowned upon and the Watchtower Society instructs its public speakers to use the NWT in their discourses.

This translation, first published in 1950 with many revisions since, is a modern language translation by an anonymous committee of men who are described in the forward of the 1984 revision as follows:

"The translators of this work, who fear and love the Divine Author of the Holy Scriptures, feel toward Him a special responsibility to transmit his thoughts and declarations as accurately as possible."

This is surely a noble and laudable aim on the part of the translation committee and one with which most Bible students would be comfortable. Unfortunately, as we will see, the resulting work is in fact the thoughts and declarations of God as interpreted by the Watchtower Society. It is typical of the arrogance of the Watchtower Society and their lack of respect for the work of other Bible scholars that they insist on using their own translation as if all others have been contaminated by "false religion."

The translation uses the Latinised form of the divine name "Jehovah" 6,828 times where the tetragrammaton (a transliteration of the four letters representing God's name in the Hebrew Bible) occurs in the Old Testament. The exact pronunciation of the name is not known as only the consonants of the name (YHWH) survive but most modern scholars today believe the probable pronunciation to be Yah' weh.[13] In addition to this, the name "Jehovah" has been *added* to the New Testament 237 times. This action has come under severe criticism by Bible Scholars as we will see.

Although the names of those involved in the translation committee have been kept secret by the Watchtower Society, Raymond Franz, himself a member of the Governing Body of Jehovah's Witnesses for nine years, has identified the committee members as: Frederick Franz, Nathan Knorr, Albert Schroeder and George Gangas. In his book "Crisis of Conscience" Raymond Franz makes this observation regarding the committee:

"Fred Franz, however, was the only one with sufficient knowledge of the Bible languages to attempt a translation of this kind. He had studied Greek for two years in the University of Cincinnati but was only self taught in Hebrew."[14]

Compare this with the efforts put into compiling the *New International Version* which drew together the skills of more than 110 Bible scholars from 34 religious groups and one wonders whether the *New World Translation* is everything that the Watchtower Society claims it to be.

While it is true that all who approach the task of Bible translation bring their own theology and must, even if only to a small degree, be guided by it in cases where the meaning of scripture is unclear, the New World Translation has received harsh criticism as a highly sectarian work. Some of these criticisms are outlined below:

Dr. Robert H Countess in his book *The Jehovah's Witnesses' New Testament* makes the following concluding comments:

"NWT has been sharply unsuccessful in keeping doctrinal considerations from influencing the actual translation... In the opinion of this investigator the *New World Translation of the Christian Greek Scriptures* must be viewed as a radically biased piece of work. At some points it is actually dishonest. At others it is neither modern nor scholarly. And interwoven throughout its fabric is inconsistent application of its own principles enunciated in the Forward and Appendix."[15]

Dr. William Barclay (University of Glasgow) is quoted in "The Expository Times" as saying:

"The deliberate distortion of truth by this sect is seen in their New Testament translations."

After referring to a particular case in point Dr. Barclay concluded:

"It is abundantly clear that a sect which can translate the New Testament like that is intellectually dishonest."[16]

What are the NWT passages that incite such strong condemnation? Obviously an in depth consideration of all the disputed verses and the scholarship behind them is beyond the scope of this text but a few examples will serve as an example.

Luke 23:43 "And he said to him: 'Truly I tell you today, You will be with me in paradise'"

This is the NWT rendering of Jesus' words to the repentant evildoer hanging along side him shortly before his death. It is the doctrinal position of the Witnesses that this evildoer did not go to heaven with

Jesus but must await a resurrection at a future time. In order for this verse to harmonise with that view, the Watchtower Society translators moved the comma in the sentence to a position after the word "today" instead of its position *before* the word "today" as it exists in the Westcott and Hort source text used in the preparation of the NWT. This radically changes the meaning of Jesus' words. Notice how this verse is rendered in other popular versions:

"Verily I say unto thee, Today shalt thou be with me in paradise" King James Version.

"I tell you the truth, today you will be with me in paradise" New International Version.

"Today you will be with me in paradise. This is a solemn promise" Living Bible.

"Truly I tell you, today you will be with me in paradise" New Revised Standard Version.

So the issue here is whether the text should be rendered as "Truly I tell you today,…" or "Truly I tell you, today…" The latter rendering contradicts Watchtower Society doctrine which insists that a resurrection to earthly life is the reward for the faithful and not an ascension to heaven immediately upon death.

The expression "Truly I tell you" or "Truly I say to you" is a figure of speech that Jesus used often in his teaching according to the Gospel accounts. It is damning evidence that in the more than seventy occasions where Jesus is recorded as using this expression in the four Gospel accounts, *only in this instance* is the comma following the expression moved to alter the meaning in the *New World Translation*. The Watchtower Society would have us believe, with no other justification other than that it conflicts with their own doctrine, that in this one instance, Jesus departed from his usual custom and said "truly I tell you *today*." Clearly, the text of the Bible has been tampered with to support the Witnesses' belief.

John 17:3 "This means everlasting life, their taking in knowledge of you, the only true God, and of the one whom you sent forth, Jesus Christ." (NWT)

This is one of the Witnesses' favourite scriptures as it seems to lend support to their claim that eternal life depends on a systematic and logical study of the Bible, a process of gaining accurate knowledge about the Bible and its meaning. Notice how the Greek is rendered in the four translations used previously:

"And this is life eternal, that they might know thee the only true God, and Jesus Christ, whom thou hast sent" King James Version.

"Now this is eternal life: that they may know you, the only true God, and Jesus Christ, whom you have sent" New International Version.

"And this is the way to have eternal life - by knowing you, the only true God, and Jesus Christ, the one you sent to earth!" Living Bible.

"And this is eternal life, that they may know you, the only true God, and Jesus Christ whom you have sent" New Revised Standard Version.

Notice the difference between these translations and the *New World Translation*. Instead of "knowing" or "Know" the Watchtower Society has rendered the original Greek as "taking in knowledge."

There is a great deal of difference in the minds of most Christians between general knowledge of the Bible and knowing God. The Greek word for "know" in this instance indicates intimacy with another person. *Vines Expository Dictionary of New Testament Words* shows that this same Greek word appears in the Bible book of Matthew chapter one verse twenty five:[17]

"*And knew her not until she had brought forth her firstborn son: and he called his name JESUS*" (KJV).

Obviously in this case the word "know" refers to sexual intercourse between Joseph and Mary and so provides an insight into the depth of the intimate personal relationship conveyed by this word. The NWT rendering of this verse favours the Witnesses' view that regular and diligent study is the key to gaining God's acceptance. It is inexcusable however, to smuggle this view into the Bible by mistranslation.

Interestingly, this same slavish study of the scripture, as required by the Witnesses, was exposed in the New Testament by Jesus as being a fault of the Jewish teachers of his day. We find his words in John 5:39 & 40

"*You diligently study the scriptures because you think that by them you possess eternal life. These are the scriptures that testify about me, yet you refuse to come to me to have life*" (NIV).

The point being made is that the religious leaders assembled great knowledge of the scriptures but it did not benefit them as they had no real relationship with

God.

Romans 14:7-9 "For none of us lives to himself alone and none of us dies to himself alone. If we live, we live to the LORD; and if we die, we die to the LORD. So, whether we live or die, we belong to the LORD. For this very reason, Christ died and returned to life so that he might be the LORD of both the dead and the living" (NIV).

The Greek word here rendered "LORD" in its four occurrences is *Kurios.*[18] In an effort to insert the Divine Name into the New Testament, the Witnesses translate this Greek word as "Jehovah." This rendering presents them with a specific problem in this passage however as the Watchtower Society teaches that the trinity doctrine is of pagan origin[19] and that "Jehovah" is the name of the Almighty God and is never applied to Jesus. Notice how the *New World Translation* interprets this passage in support of the Witnesses' own doctrine:

"None of us, in fact, lives with regard to himself only, and no one dies with regard to himself only; for both if we live, we live to Jehovah, and if we die, we die to Jehovah. Therefore both if we live and if we die, we belong to Jehovah. For to this end Christ died and came to life again, that he might be Lord over both the dead and the living."

By rendering the same Greek root *Kurios* as "Jehovah" in the first three instances but then as "Lord" in the last one, the Witnesses create a logical *non-sequitur.* Verse nine that discusses Jesus, no longer follows logically from the preceding thought, it appears as though two separate identities are discussed in this passage. The text is now twisted into supporting the doctrine of the Witnesses.

To translate the final occurrence of *Kurios* as "Jehovah" would imply that Jesus was Jehovah, which would be anathema to the Witnesses, and so the text is manipulated to reveal something different, a meaning that is consistent with the Witnesses' theology.

The attempt by the Witnesses to smuggle the name "Jehovah" into the New Testament as they have done 237 times in the NWT has brought strong opposition. Many commentators see this as attempt to Judaize the NT, diminish the role of Christ and avoid confusion that may lend support to the trinity doctrine.

The Watchtower Society itself admits that: "no early surviving Greek manuscript of the 'New Testament' contains the personal name of God."[20] To justify the insertion of the name they cite more recent translations of New Testament portions into Hebrew, the very oldest of which is dated 1385 and many are much younger.

A detailed discussion of the Watchtower Society's methods is contained in the book *The Jehovah's Witnesses and the New Testament* by Dr. Robert H Countess who concludes his examination with the words:

"The 'restoration' of the Divine Name is a misnomer and ought rather to be designated the *'insertion'* of the Divine Name.""[21] (italics in original)

Many other examples could be cited to show that the Witnesses' theology guided the translation that constitutes their primary text. Two verses of the Gospel of John (John 1:1 and John 8:58) have even formed the basis of an entire book.[22] These few examples however, should be sufficient to cast doubt over the reliability of the New World Translation.

It is one thing to debate the meanings and subtleties of a particular Bible verse, but it is an altogether different and more serious matter when the Scriptures are actually tampered with to superimpose a particular doctrine on them. The Bible, which serves as the cornerstone of Christian belief deserves greater respect.

In this the Watchtower Society demonstrates a subtle ambiguity. In the first instance, the Society claims that the Bible has been handed down faithfully to our generation without the passage of time and translation eroding the true meaning and message. Despite this, we are then told that we need a special translation of the Bible if we are to realise the complete truth and have confidence in the written word. It appears to my mind at least, the height of arrogance that the Watchtower Society holds in such low esteem the diligent efforts of Bible scholars over many centuries that they feel the need to publish their own translation and then praise it so thoroughly.

The point is well made by David Reed in his book *Jehovah's Witnesses answered Verse by Verse:*

"This is a situation in which individual JW's do not need to twist Scripture to fit the doctrines they have been taught - the verse comes already pre-twisted in their own Bible."[23]

Let Thy Kingdom Come

"I have lived in this world just long enough
to look carefully the second time
into things that I am the most certain
of the first time."

Josh Billings

We have discussed in the previous chapter the belief held by Jehovah's Witnesses that the world's end is nigh. In this chapter I would like to outline the reasons why they continue to hold this opinion and examine the evidence they offer for its support.

Much of the urgency with which the Witnesses conduct their preaching work stems from their conviction that mankind is now living in the time of the end. They pinpoint this time by reference to several Bible prophecies and the interpretation of their fulfilment. In my own case, my father, encouraged by the teachings of the Watchtower Society, sold the family home in 1972 and gave up his job. Like so many other Witnesses he was certain that the world would end in 1975 and so marched up the metaphorical mountain in anticipation.

Readers may need to fortify themselves before tackling this chapter. It involves some of the most unfathomable thought processes and logical contortions imaginable.

The Times of the Nations

The Bible book of Daniel is where we must begin our examination of prophecy. Chapter four of Daniel recounts an event said to have been experienced by Nebuchadnezzar, king of Babylonia from 602 BC.[1] The Bible narrative tells of the King's haughty attitude as he strolls around his grand palace, boasting of his own might and prosperity. From all accounts he had much to boast about. Nebuchadnezzar presided over a massive building campaign throughout Babylon. The city spanned the Euphrates river and was surrounded by a seventeen kilometre outer wall enclosing suburbs and the King's summer palace. The inner wall was wide enough to permit two chariots abreast.

Entrance to the city was through eight gates, the most famous of which, the northern Ishtar gate, is decorated with reliefs of dragons and bulls in enamelled brick. The city contained the "Hanging

Gardens of Babylon," one of the seven wonders of the ancient world as well as many temples lavishly decorated with gold.

One can imagine Nebuchadnezzar's boastful pride as he contemplates the majesty of his city. In the story, at this very moment he is struck by God and becomes as a beast, eating vegetation like a bull and becoming wild in appearance. This event had been prophesied in the book of Daniel by reference to a mighty tree. So mighty was this tree that its top was in the heavens and it was visible from the entire earth (assuming the earth was flat of course). The prophecy said that the tree would be cut down but its rootstock left in the ground with a banding of iron and copper to prevent its growth for a predetermined period of time. This period of time was designated as "seven times" although the length of the "times" were not specified. After the seven times had run their course, the banding would be removed allowing the tree to grow again.

The Bible account makes the application for us, showing that the king himself was the mighty tree and his period of madness was represented by the tree's time of restricted growth. After the "seven times" had passed the king was restored to his former glory but with a more humble attitude toward the God of the Jews.

An interesting story perhaps, but what has this to do with the end of the world? Well, it is this very prophecy that Jehovah's Witnesses use to demonstrate that God's Kingdom was established invisibly in the year 1914. How do they arrive at this conclusion? They do so by analysing several of the key elements in the prophecy and by assigning special meaning to these elements which extend the prophecy beyond its initial and obvious application to the king of Babylon.

Firstly the Witnesses contend that trees are used in the Bible to represent governments, ruling powers, and kingdoms[2] and therefore claim that the tree of Daniel chapter four, which is endowed with majestic proportions by the Bible writer, and the prophecy concerning it actually has application to the Kingdom of God.[3]

The "seven times" then, during which period the tree was banded, refer to a period in man's history when God was not ruling in an active way. The unbinding of the tree would signify a return or a restoration of God's rulership. All we need to establish therefore is the point in history when the "times" started running and their duration to know when the kingdom of God would be re-established over earth. Unfortunately for the detectives among us the trail becomes blurred at this point and if we have not already done so we must now suspend our disbelief for what follows.

Step one, therefore, is to determine the length of the "times."

There is another book of the Bible that mentions the concept of "times" and that is the last book of the Bible, Revelation. This book has confounded religious scholars for centuries as it is written in symbolic, and on occasion, horrific language. Nevertheless, the Watchtower Society will point out that the Greek word for "times" is *kairous*[4] which can refer to a set and fixed period of time the length of which, according to their interpretation, we can deduce from Revelation.

The section of the book of Revelation in question is chapter twelve. Here we find a symbolic drama taking place between a fiery coloured, seven headed dragon and the Archangel Michael.[5] The dragon's endeavour is to devour the newly born child of the third character of the drama, a woman "clothed with the sun and with the moon under her feet and upon her head a crown of twelve stars."

At this point in the proceedings the woman flees to the wilderness where she is fed by God for "a time and times and half a time." So here we have the mysterious concept of "times" referred to again. However, on this occasion the event is repeated in the same chapter of Revelation with the time period given as "a thousand two hundred and sixty days." We now have a way of measuring the length of the "times" by comparing the same period expressed in the Bible in two different ways. If three and a half times (time, times and half a time) equal 1260 days, then the seven times from Daniel chapter four must equal (1260 X 2) or 2520 days!

Finally it appears that we are getting somewhere. It seems we could apply this precise measurement of each "time" to the prophecy in Daniel chapter four which launched us into this chronological crusade. This of course, is conditional on our allowing the "times" of Daniel and the "times" of Revelation, two books written over six hundred years apart, to be remotely connected let alone representing the same number of days, but let us not be side-tracked after making so much progress.

The next thing we need to know, explain the Witnesses, is when the clock started running. That is, when the "seven times" of Daniel began. If the tree represents God's government, then we need to look for the time God's government over the earth was chopped down so to speak. The Witnesses will tell us that we need look no further than the destruction of Jerusalem (representing God's throne) by the Babylonians. This event would mark the beginning of the "seven times."

Unfortunately, here we hit a snag. The date of Jerusalem's destruction given in all Witness literature is 607 BC.[6] Awkwardly, this date conflicts with the rest of the world's historians who locate the destruction as taking place in 587/586 BC.[7] This latter date is supported from multiple streams of secular history, including tens of thousands of clay cuneiform tablets found in the Mesopotamia area dating back to the time of ancient Babylon.

The Witnesses hold to their date because it is established by another Bible prophecy[8] and to permit the 587/586 BC date would be to acknowledge that either this other Bible prophecy was inaccurate or it has been interpreted incorrectly. At this point I hope you will allow me to spare us both the pain of discussing this other prophecy but suffice it to say that there is not one shred of evidence to suggest that Jerusalem's destruction occurred in 607 BC.

It is interesting at this point to note the words of Raymond Franz, himself a former member of the executive council or governing body of Jehovah's

Witnesses for nine years. In his book *Crisis of Conscience* he writes, concerning the preparation of a new Witness Bible dictionary:

"Months of research were spent on this one subject of 'Chronology' and it resulted in the longest article in the *Aid* publication. Much of the time was spent endeavouring to find some proof, some backing in history, for the 607 BCE date so crucial to our calculations for 1914... We found absolutely nothing in support of 607 BCE. All historians pointed to a date twenty years later."[9]

So the Watchtower Society publish their interpretation, which pivots on the date of 607 BC, with the full knowledge that it conflicts with *all* secular historical accounts.

Let us return however to the prophecy of the "seven times." Now we have a starting date (or two dates in fact). So if we count forward 2520 days from the destruction of Jerusalem in the year 607 BC (or 587/586 BC for that matter) what do we find? Nothing. Nothing of note took place 2520 days after either 607 BC or 587/586 BC.[10]

In order to project these "seven times" into the future, the Witnesses now invoke what they describe as "The Prophetic Rule." Basically this describes the practice of substituting a day for a year, just as the Israelites had to wander in the wilderness for forty years as penance for the forty days that the Israelite spies took to bring back their bad report on the land of Canaan.[11]

Quite what makes this divine judgement upon the Jews a prophetic "rule" or even allowing it to be so, what necessitates its application in this case is not said, however if you have followed the discussion so far, this small detail will be of no trouble to you. The convenient part is that by the application of this alleged "rule," we are now dealing with a period of 2520 years instead of days. What took place 2520 years after 607 BC? Allowing that there was no year zero we come to the year 1914. Here at last is a date of significance.

All of these difficulties notwithstanding, this is the torturous process the Witnesses employ to locate 1914 as the date God's Kingdom was reinstalled. Obviously human governments continued to rule in, and subsequent to, the year 1914, but the Watchtower Society was undeterred by this mere bagatelle. As we have seen, in constructing this interpretation they perpetrate much violence on the scriptural texts involved as well as the established history of civilisation.

Of course we also need to remind ourselves that historians would place the destruction of Jerusalem in the year 587/586 BC which would bring us to the considerably less significant time of approximately 1935. It is a little known fact among Witnesses that this chronology did not originate with the Watchtower Society. John Aquila Brown developed almost identical chronology and published his conclusions complete with the "seven times" and 2520 years in the year 1823 *which was twenty nine years before Watchtower founder Russell was born!*

It was Russell's association with N.H. Barbour, a Second Adventist who had studied the work of Brown that led him to adopt the same chronology and arrive at the 1914 date.[12]

So we have used Witness chronology to find the end of the "seven times" when God's rule would begin again over mankind. One could be forgiven for thinking that this might coincide with a reign of peace on the earth instead of the first world war and in fact the Witnesses themselves expected to be caught away in the rapture at that time.[13] Finding that their feet remained firmly planted on the ground however, demanded a re-think.

The Second Coming

The Watchtower Society examined the Greek word translated in the Bible by the English word "coming" (they had expected Christ's coming in 1914). The Greek word in question is *parousia*.[14] One meaning for this noun is "being alongside" and it can be used to refer more to a person's presence than their arrival. Seizing upon this meaning, the Witnesses speculated that it would be more sensible to seek signs of Christ's presence than to look for his coming.

Just as one's presence is measured by a period of time while one's coming happens in an instant of time, they retrospectively concluded that Christ in 1914 would begin a period of invisible rule that would constitute his presence until he took action toward this world. The Watchtower Society's interpretation sidesteps many difficulties of course, not the least of which is the fact that *parousia* has a number of subtle shades of meaning which do not limit its usage to "presence."

The time in which we now live, say the Witnesses, is that very period.[15] As each year progresses to its conclusion we are closer to the divine judgement. Because no one knows when that day will be, the preaching of the Kingdom message must be completed with urgency and to the extent of each member's ability. It appears, in fact, that this Kingdom extends its rule over the Witnesses exclusively as they alone recognise its existence.

The Witnesses are fond of pointing out that the Watchtower Society looked forward to 1914 for many years before it arrived, demonstrating to their minds at least that God used the Society to foretell future events in relation to his purpose. In this context, however, we must remember that the 1914 date has represented differing things to the Witnesses over the years. As just mentioned, the current view is that Christ has been invisibly ruling since 1914.

However, although thinking that 1914 would mark the end of "the times of the nations," the date 1874 was seen at one time to be the beginning of Christ's invisible presence, with 1914 marking the time by which Jesus would have taken over all rulership from the world's political powers.[16] So instead of 1914 marking a beginning of something significant in Witness chronology, for decades it marked the end of a period of significance for them.

1918 & 1920

As 1914 came and went Rutherford arranged to have published a book entitled *The Finished Mystery* following Russell's death in 1916. This publication shone new light on the years 1918 and 1920. In this work we find the following event scheduled to occur:

"Also, in the year 1918, when God destroys the churches wholesale and the church members by millions, it shall be that any that escape shall come to the works of Pastor Russell to learn the meaning of the downfall of "Christianity."[17]

And with respect to world governments:

"Even the republics will disappear in the fall of 1920... Every kingdom of earth will pass away, be swallowed up in anarchy."[18]

Of course these dates slipped past with slightly less insurrection than the faithful had hoped.

1925

In 1920 the president of the Watchtower society J.F. Rutherford published a booklet entitled *Millions now living will never die* This was tied to the new date of 1925.

The booklet made the following prophecy:

"Therefore we may confidently expect that 1925 will mark the return of Abraham, Isaac, Jacob and the faithful prophets of old, particularly those named by the Apostle in Hebrews chapter eleven, to the condition of human perfection."[19]

This date was confirmed by other Watchtower publications. In fact the organisation went so far as to acquire a property in San Diego California and to build a house known as Beth-Sarim (house of Princes) to accommodate the resurrected faithful men of old. It was here that Rutherford eventually died in 1942 after which the property was quietly sold.

The second world war

The Watchtower society clearly expected World War II to end in the battle of Armageddon (the complete destruction of the wicked by God) as the following extracts from its publications establish

Showing that a decisive victory for either side was not allowed by Bible prophecy, the *Watchtower* magazine of December 15 1941 reported:

"Will the present world conflict between the 'Axis Powers' and the so called 'democracies,' the opposers, end in a decisive victory for either side? the prophecy indicates the contrary result."[20]

And then linking the end of Nazi rule with the end of demon rule (and thus a start to God's rule), we discover the prophecy:

"Thus the end for ever of Nazi-Fascist-Hierarchy rule will come, and that will mark the end for ever of demon rule."[21]

The booklet *Judge Rutherford Uncovers Fifth Column*

published in 1940 reported:

"At a public address in London, which was transmitted throughout the British Empire, and was delivered in 1938, I stated that the Nazis and Fascists were bent on destroying the British Empire, and that that would be accomplished."[22]

As if to create even more expectation in the minds of the readers, the *Watchtower* of September 15 1941 used the expression:

"in the remaining months before Armageddon" when discussing the Lord's work.[23]

These quotations show unquestionably that the Witnesses expected the war to lead on into Armageddon. Once again the prophecies of their organisation were misleading.

1975

The Watchtower Society was neither deterred nor humbled by its dismal record of failed prophecy to date. Attempting to pinpoint more precisely when the Divine judgement would arrive, the Witnesses again delved into chronology. It had been proposed (based on pure speculation) that the creative days from the Bible book of Genesis were of 7000 years duration. Because the Bible spoke of the seventh day as concluding with a thousand year reign of peace, all one had to do, reasoned the Witnesses, was to find out when the seventh day began, count forward 6000 years and hence locate the date for the beginning of the millennial reign of Christ. The "seventh day" of creation was held to have begun when God rested from his creative work after forming the man Adam from the dust of the ground. Thus began the process of adding up all the generations of the Bible. This is a very dubious practice as one has to assume at the outset that the incredible ages of the ancient Bible characters (930 years in the case of Adam) were literal or used the same units of measure as we today.

The *Evangelical Dictionary of Theology* by Elwell - 1984 comments on this approach:

"As to the biblical genealogies, noted OT scholar W.H. Green, a contributor to the famous *Fundamentals* papers, analysed these and concluded that they were not intended and cannot be legitimately used to construct a chronology."[24]

Despite such notes of caution, the Witnesses forged ahead and the date of 4026 BC was established as marking the year of Adam's creation. Once again counting forward 6000 years brought us to the year 1975 and this became the date of focus during the sixties and early seventies.[25] This date was to mark the beginning of Christ's thousand year reign of peace. Many Witnesses made drastic life style changes including selling their houses before this year arrived (as did my father) so that they could use the proceeds to fund full time preaching. Unfortunately for them, the year passed unremarkably.

It should also be noted that once again the language used in the publications of the Watchtower Society created an air of expectation and excitement among the Witnesses.

For example, an article entitled "How are you

using your life" appeared in the May 1974 edition of the *Kingdom Ministry*, a monthly booklet for Witnesses only. The piece asserted:

"Reports are heard of brothers selling their homes and property and planning to finish out the rest of their days in this old system in the Pioneer (full-time) Service. *Certainly this is a fine way to spend the short time remaining* before the wicked world's end."[26] (italics added)

So rather than cautioning the faithful against such a risky course of action, the Watchtower Society acted irresponsibly and actually praised such injudicious action.

The *Watchtower* magazine was also used to stimulate anticipation among the faithful. As only one example of many, consider the May 1 1968 edition which opined:

"The immediate future is certain to be filled with climactic events, for this old system is nearing its complete end. *Within a few years at most* the final parts of Bible prophecy relative to these "last days" will undergo fulfilment, resulting in the liberation of surviving mankind into Christ's glorious 1,000 year reign. What difficult days, but, at the same time, what grand days are just ahead."[27] (italics added)

At the time of writing twenty six years have elapsed since these words were penned, this surely aggrandises the meaning of the word "few."

The most disturbing statement of all appeared in the August 15 1968 edition of the *Watchtower* magazine. Those familiar with the Gospel accounts will remember that Christians were given a caution by none other than Christ himself concerning speculation about the coming of the "Lord's day." The organisation in effect instructed the Witnesses to put more faith in its own unique chronology than the words of Jesus himself. The article stated:

"One thing is absolutely certain, Bible chronology reinforced with fulfilled Bible prophecy shows that six thousand years of man's existence will soon be up, yes, within this generation! (Matt. 24:34) This is, therefore, no time to be indifferent or complacent. This is not the time to be toying with the words of Jesus that "concerning that day and hour *nobody* knows, neither the angels of the Heavens nor the Son, but only the Father." (Matt 24:36) To the contrary, it is a time when one should be keenly aware that the end of this system of things is rapidly coming to its violent end. Make no mistake, it is sufficient that the Father himself *knows* both the "day and the hour!"[28] (italics in original)

So although Jesus cautioned his followers not to focus on a specific date or time, the Watchtower Society overruled that caution in an effort to create a sense of urgency among the Witnesses which served to influence the decisions that many individuals made regarding their future. The outcome, of course, was that the total number of hours spent by Witnesses in the public preaching increased dramatically in proportion to their heightened expectation. This increase was then fed back into the Watchtower propaganda machine as an interpretation of God's blessing on the work in the short time remaining before the end.

Animated by this process it is no wonder that great anticipation existed among Jehovah's Witnesses at that time followed by equally great disappointment when the world's end did not eventuate.

However, we are not done yet.

In an effort to salvage the situation, the Watchtower Society admitted to making a mistake. The seventh day was indeed God's day of resting from creation. But he did not rest after creating Adam because the Bible tells us that Adam was alone in the garden of Eden for some time. No, God rested, according to Genesis, after he created Eve.[29] So the undetermined period of time that Adam lived alone in Eden accounted for the difference between the year 1975 and the beginning of the Millennial reign! As at the time of writing it is now 1994, this means that Adam was at least nineteen years in the garden of Eden looking for a mate. It then is no surprise that he reacted in the way the Bible describes when introduced to Eve![30]

We should not overlook the fact that there is no basis whatever to assume the creative days of Genesis equate to 7000 year time periods in the first place or indeed any time periods. Nor does it seem reasonable to assume that the fantastic ages recorded in the book of Genesis are to be taken literally. Without these assumptions however, the chronology of the Witnesses becomes even more fanciful.

New enlightenment notwithstanding, it remains that 1975 turned out to be a fizzer where end-of-the-world action was concerned. Who takes the responsibility for all of this erroneous instruction and false hope? Does the organisation that claims to be God's channel shoulder the blame? In a pattern that appears to have continued from the founding of the Watchtower Society, the individual Witness members are held to be at fault. The *Watchtower* magazine of July 15 1976 carried this message:

"It is not advisable for us to set our sights on a certain date... if anyone has been disappointed through not following this line of thought, he should now concentrate on adjusting his viewpoint, seeing that it was not the word of God that failed or deceived him and brought disappointment, *but that his own understanding was based on wrong premises.*"[31] (italics added)

Yet who led the followers in their thinking? The Watchtower Society itself! What a callous and cynical attitude to display toward those who sold their homes and were commended for doing so, only to find themselves financially disadvantaged and emotionally damaged as a result.

It seems, in fact, to be the general opinion now among the majority of Witnesses that the Watchtower Society never actually said the world would end in 1975, and that many individuals simply "read into" the Society's statements things that were not there. A re-examination of the previous quotes will reveal that if not actually spelling out the end in 1975, it was without a doubt strongly implied. With such a history of failed dates one would think the Watchtower Society should have erred on the side of caution in this case instead of building false expectations and commending the rash acts of individual Witnesses. In this the society remains culpable.

The Watchtower society has also attempted to cover over this embarrassing episode in subsequent reprints of their publications. Here are two examples:

In 1968 the Watchtower Society published a book entitled *The Truth that leads to Eternal Life*. This publication became the principle tool used in teaching prospective Witnesses and by 1982 over 100 million copies had been printed. In 1981 however, a new edition was quietly released. Why? because of damaging references in the original edition to 1975 such as these words on page 9:

"Also, as reported back in 1960, a former United States Secretary of State, Dean Acheson, declared that our time is "a period of unequalled instability, unequalled violence." And he warned: "I know enough of what is going on to assure you that, in fifteen years from today, this world is going to be too dangerous to live in."

Fifteen years from 1960 was of course 1975 and although this quote served the Witnesses well before 1975, after that year it was an embarrassment. Notice how this reference appeared in the 1981 edition of the book:

"Also, as reported back in 1960, a former United States Secretary of State, Dean Acheson, declared that our time is "a period of unequalled instability, unequalled violence." Based on what he knew was then going on in the world, it was his conclusion that soon "this world is going to be too dangerous to live in."

Clearly the attempt is to shield the organisation from accusations regarding the imprudent statements made concerning 1975.

There is evidence to suggest also that the *Watchtower Publications Index (1930-1960)* which replaced previous indexes continued this dishonest practice of omitting references that may prove damaging to the organisation for anyone using it to search through the society's literature.[32]

The Last Days

The Witnesses have more than just chronology up their spiritual sleeves however. The deterioration in the world's affairs in modern times takes on a special meaning for them. They look closely at Jesus' prophecy regarding the first century city of Jerusalem and uncover special meaning for our day.

The Gospel accounts relate how Jesus warned his followers that Jerusalem would be surrounded by an encamped army and eventually destroyed.[33] His disciples were anxious to know when this would happen and in response to their questioning, Jesus gave them a complex sign to look for. He mentioned wars and famines, earthquakes and great signs in the heavens. By this the disciples would know that the end was close and that Jesus' coming was nigh.[34]

History tells us that the city and temple of Jerusalem were destroyed in the year 70 AD by the Roman armies after a siege of some duration.[35] No historian however, recorded earthquakes or great signs in the sky at this time. In fact several aspects of Jesus' prophecy were not fulfilled. From this the

Witnesses deduce that the prophecy must have a greater fulfilment in modern times.[36] As they had already established, Christ had begun to reign invisibly in the year 1914 and so they determined that this prophecy must therefore refer to our very day.

Hence the worsening world condition is seen as proof that we are in the "last days" of which Jesus spoke and the earthquakes, famines and wars are a fulfilment of the sign Jesus gave.[37] Needless to say, the Watchtower Society keep these disasters close to the minds and hearts of the faithful. This highlights once again the need for urgency regarding their preaching work because we are now eighty years into the time of the end and surely must be close to the end of the end.

"This Generation"

After describing the signs that would indicate his presence, Jesus remarked to his disciples that this generation (the one witnessing the signs) would not pass away until all of his words were fulfilled.[38] Some have suggested that a Bible generation is forty years and so this statement refers to the suffering of the last generation. At this time Jesus was in his early thirties and the city of Jerusalem was destroyed less than forty years later so if we accept that Jesus was accurately quoted here then he was correct.

The Witnesses, of course, locate the major fulfilment of this prophecy in our day. So then, who comprise the generation of whom Jesus spoke? The

Witnesses explain this to be the generation that saw the events surrounding the invisible return of Christ in 1914, which same generation will still be alive to see the end occur. They have further stated that those alive in 1914 must have been old enough to appreciate what was happening in the world at that time.[39]

Here we seem to have a problem. If we allow that, in order to understand the events taking place in 1914, a person would have to be a teenager at least, (let us say fifteen years old for the sake of the argument) then the 1914 generation is getting on in years. Just to make it more difficult, the translation of the Bible that the Witnesses have produced for themselves differs from the King James version in the rendition of this particular scripture. Their translation has Jesus saying that:

"…this generation *will by no means* pass away until all things occur"[40] (italics added).

The implication in this rendition is that a considerable number of persons from the 1914 generation would still be alive when the end came.

With the benefit of hindsight we are able to look back on the way this has been presented over the years in the organisation's publications. We see a stretching of "this generation" as time progresses. This can be illustrated by the following extracts:

The *Awake!* magazine of October 8 1968 carried this view:

"Jesus was obviously speaking about those who were old enough to witness with understanding what took place when the "last days" began... Even if we presume that *youngsters 15 years of age* would be perceptive enough to realize the import of what happened in 1914, it would still make the youngest of "this generation" nearly 70 years old today... Jesus said that the end of this wicked world would come before that generation passed away in death."[41] (italics added)

Twelve years later the *Watchtower* gave this modified view in its October 15 1980 edition:

"It is the generation of people that saw the catastrophic events that broke forth in connection with World War I from 1914 onward... *If you assume that 10 is the age at which an event creates a lasting impression*"[42] (italics added) Here the age is reduced from 15 to 10 years to stretch another five years out of the dying generation.

Again four years later in the Watchtower magazine of May 15 1984:

"If Jesus used 'generation' in that sense and we apply it to 1914, then *the babies of that generation are now 70 years old or older*... Some of them 'will by no means pass away until all these things occur.'"[43] (italics added)

Here we see clearly demonstrated, the Witness practice of retrospectively altering the doctrine to fit the circumstances. The age of those witnessing the events of 1914 has been progressively reduced from fifteen years to "babies." It would appear that the Watchtower Society have wrung everything possible out of this "1914" generation. In doing so they have stretched to the limit the doctrine which most significantly sets them apart from all other religious groups.

As an individual born in 1914 is eighty years old at the time of writing, it seems that in this instance the Witnesses are hoist on their own petard. I wait with interest to see how they will extricate themselves from this predicament.

** Author's note. With the benefit of hindsight we need wait no longer to discover how this was resolved. In April 2010, the doctrinal sleight of hand for which the Witnesses are renowned was again in evidence as the Watchtower magazine explained:

"Although we cannot measure the exact length of this generation, we do well to keep in mind several things about the word generation: It usually refers to people of varying ages whose lives overlap during a particular time period; it is not excessively long; and it has an end. (Ex. 1:6) How, then, are we to understand Jesus words about this generation? He evidently meant that the lives of the anointed who were on hand when the sign began to become evident in 1914 would overlap with the lives of other anointed ones who would see the start of the great tribulation."

So now the duration of "this generation" has been made equivalent to two overlapping generations, buying some precious wriggle room for everyone. An alternative and more logical explanation might be that Jesus' words have no specific relevance to any generation in our modern times and that the Watchtower Society simply got it wrong.

Peace and Security

Another   interesting   prophecy   to   which   the

Witnesses give much attention is contained in the Apostle Paul's first letter to the Christians in the Greek city of Thessalonica. In this letter Paul encourages vigilance regarding the destruction foretold by Jesus. As this letter is said to have been written approximately fifteen or twenty years before the destruction of Jerusalem, it may have served as a timely warning.

As we have said, the Witnesses locate the fulfilment of all these "last days" prophecies in our time and so for them these words of Paul also apply now. The text they focus upon is Paul's warning that:

"whenever they say 'peace and security' then sudden destruction is to be instantly upon them."[44]

So for the Witnesses, another sign to look for as the world's end approaches is a claim of world peace. If we combine this "peace and security cry" with the woes that Jesus predicted would mark the last days, we have an interesting phenomenon. As the Witnesses look into the world news for proof that we live in the last days, whatever they find serves their purpose! If the news is of violence and war, (as with the Gulf wars for example) then Jesus' sign is being fulfilled. If the news shows peace breaking out (such as with the downing of the Berlin wall) then the apostle Paul's words are ringing in their ears. Whichever way the world goes it strengthens the Witnesses' faith in Watchtower prophecy.

It has been my experience that the capacity possessed by some Witnesses to fit world events into one of these two categories, year after year, is nothing short of amazing. The words of George Bernard

Shaw synopsize their position:

"The fact that a believer is happier than a sceptic is no more to the point than the fact that a drunken man is happier than a sober one. The happiness of credulity is a cheap and dangerous quality."

The United Nations

The Witnesses identify key players in the global drama acted out before them. One of these is the United Nations Organisation. To see where it fits in to this complex picture, we must return to Jesus' words concerning the destruction of Jerusalem.

The Gospel account of Matthew tells us that Jesus had another warning for his disciples. He urged them to look out for:

"*the disgusting thing that causes desolation....standing in a holy place.*"[45]

This would be proof positive that his words were being fulfilled. Many Bible commentators identify this "disgusting thing" with the Roman armies under General Titus. They were standing in a holy place when they ransacked the temple in Jerusalem.

If we locate the fulfilment of this prophecy in our day, as the Watchtower Society would have us do, who or what is "the disgusting thing" and where is the "holy place" in which it stands? Let us remind ourselves at this point that for the Witnesses, God has been ruling invisibly in the heavens since the year 1914. During the intervening period, have the nations of this earth submitted to that heavenly rule? Hardly. Do the nations of the world look to that kingdom to solve the difficulties between men? Once again the answer is no.

Where do they look for unification and conflict settlement? To the United Nations of course. So in this sense, the U.N. is standing in a "holy place," that is to say it's occupying the position in the eyes of mankind that properly belongs to the invisible kingdom of God.[46] So it is that the U.N. comes to play a vital role in the end of the world as we will see in chapter four.

This of course presents us with a paradox. According to the Genesis account of man's history, it was God himself that confused the languages of man during the building of the tower of Babel and thus effectively separated mankind into national groups. The resultant disunity is held against the nations by the Witnesses who are fond of pointing out the difficulties caused by such partisan quarrelling. However, when the nations attempt to construct a mechanism such as the U.N. to promote cooperation between countries, they are condemned by the Watchtower Society's interpretation of Bible prophecy.

A New World Order

As we have said, there is to be a thousand year reign of peace on the earth. Before this can take place however, all those who will not submit to the invisible kingdom of God now reigning must be destroyed. We can only presume that this includes all who are not Jehovah's Witnesses or favourably disposed toward them.

During this thousand year period, it is the work of the survivors (0.3% as we have estimated) to undo all of mankind's damage to the earth. This means that all of the world's cities have to be razed to the ground and a paradise created. The Witnesses in their publications are fond of showing images such as a man on a tractor ploughing the rubble of the old society into the ground. It seems to me that this task has been greatly oversimplified.

Imagine the project of removing the cities of New York, Los Angeles, London, Munich, Tokyo, Paris, Rome and the like, from the face of the earth by 0.3% of the population, using tractors! Many insurmountable problems spring to mind. Where will the fuel come from to power the equipment for a thousand years with all the world's refineries off line? How will the survivors deal with the nuclear reactors around the globe? Who among the Witnesses are qualified to dismantle them and what will be done with the radioactive material?

Where does one put the billions of tons of rubble remaining? How will the work effort be coordinated without the use of electricity, as all of the world's power generating stations will have no staff to run them. This means no computers, no phones, no radio or television, no lighting or power tools.

What will happen to the almost seven billion dead bodies that will be found in every apartment block and office tower and supermarket, indeed will litter every corner of the earth? What is to be done with the estimated four hundred million cars in the world? What of the arsenal of weapons possessed by all nations including nuclear, chemical and biological warheads? How does one go about wrecking fortified buildings such as Fort Knox or the many nuclear strike-proof military bunkers? The greatest tractor in the history of civilisation is hardly likely to make much of an impression on a building protecting its occupants by twenty feet of reinforced concrete. Intractable difficulties such as these are endless.

The Witnesses are quick to recognise that their task is a daunting one and are comfortable in appealing to God for assistance. It seems strange to me however, that God would give them such an assignment in the first instance, realising that they have no possible chance of completing it.

Let us with a mighty gulp swallow the scenario so far. What then at the end of the thousand years of peace?

The Final Test

Once more the Witnesses would have us explore the complex and mysterious book of Revelation. It seems that there is unfinished business to be attended. At the time when the majority of mankind perished, the Devil, say the Witnesses, was restricted in his activity but not killed outright. The book of Revelation now tells us that he is to be let loose again for one final test.[47] As if the end of the world survivors have not endured enough.

No sooner have they finished ploughing in the four hundred millionth car than the devil is let loose again. The Bible narrative used by the Witnesses tells us that the devil is successful in misleading nations to the four corners of the earth.[48] The number of people now taking a stand against God is like the sand of the sea.[49] One can imagine the looks on the faces of the faithful as they contemplate another global clean-up.

This has always appeared, to my way of thinking, a particularly complex and cruel way to settle the issue of good and evil. As with so many of these misanthropic doctrines, the freedom of the few is secured by the death of the many. Whether this presents a problem to the individual conscience seems to me to depend to a large extent on whether the individual is of the many or the few.

An Excusive Club

"There is no tariff so injurious as that with which
sectarian bigotry guards its commodities.
It dwarfs the soul by shutting out truths from
other continents of thought
and checks the circulation of its own."

Edwin Hubbell Chapin

What evidence do Jehovah's Witnesses furnish to
prove that they alone have the true religion? What is
to become of the hundreds of other Christian faiths
that now exist throughout the world? Where do all of
the non-Christian religions fit into the picture?

In this chapter I will attempt to furnish the
Witnesses' answer to these questions and to examine
their claim to be the only true faith. I will also
appraise the men that shaped the organisation

together with their bizarre beliefs and prophecies.

One lord, one faith

At the outset, the question must be asked, is there only one true faith? Is it reasonable to think that out of all the religions of mankind, only one has the absolute truth and the rest are false? It would appear to my mind that most religions have features which commend them and most fundamental faiths seem to have some unique doctrine that their adherents claim sets them apart from the rest.

The Witness perspective however, is that there is only one true religion and all the rest are under the control of the Devil.[1] The Bible book of Revelation is again used to support this view. When expanding on their belief in the existence of only one true religion, the Witnesses often cite as an example the Bible account of Noah's flood. Did not God rescue only one group of people from the deluge they ask. And further, in the Old Testament, did not God choose only one nation to be his special people? Therefore, conclude the Witnesses, we should expect to find only one true faith today. We will examine this reasoning more closely in chapter ten but I state it briefly here in an effort to develop the Watchtower Society's argument to its logical (?) conclusion.

Having established that God has always used one group of people in preference to the majority, the quest simply becomes to identify the true from the false.

Babylon the Great

Some of the more colourful language of the book of Revelation is reserved for the character described in chapter 17. I will include verses 3 to 6:

"So he carried me away in the spirit into the wilderness and I saw a woman sit upon a scarlet coloured beast, full of names of blasphemy, having seven heads and ten horns. And the woman was arrayed in purple and decked with gold and precious stones and pearls, having a golden cup in her hand full of abominations and filthiness of her fornication. And upon her forehead was a name written, mystery, Babylon the Great, the mother of the harlots and abominations of the earth. And I saw the woman drunken with the blood of the saints, and with the martyrs of Jesus, and when I saw her, I wondered with great admiration." (KJV)

Strong language indeed. To whom or what does this woman refer? While this has been a subject of debate among religious men for centuries, for the Witnesses the picture is clear. By a simplistic process of elimination they conclude that the woman represents religion itself. Not all religion of course, simply all religion except the true one.[2] It logically follows then, that with such condemnatory language used to describe this woman, God must indeed hate false religion with a passion. This composite symbol of all false religion includes not only Christian religion but every faith known to man but one, Jehovah's Witnesses themselves. With an interpretation such as this, it will come as no surprise to find that intolerance toward other religious groups has always been a characteristic of the Watchtower Society.

Although it is true that many religions have differing and sometimes conflicting views, it would appear to me the height of arrogance for a tiny group of people to classify themselves as the only religious organisation acceptable to God. To regard the sincerely held faith of every other religious person as worthy of the above description in Revelation is surely to have tunnel vision in the extreme.

What is to become of these other faiths as represented by Revelation's filthy harlot? In graphic language the seventeenth chapter of Revelation describes her demise as she is eaten alive by a ferocious wild beast.[3] Who in our modern day is represented by this beast? In the Witness interpretation it is none other than the United Nations Organisation discussed in the previous chapter.[4]

The end of earth's wickedness therefore begins with the complete desolation of all religion (Witnesses excepted of course) by the organisation charged with protecting world peace. One can only begin to imagine what the result of any such action would be. Do those among the Witnesses who ponder over these things really imagine that this could take place in countries such as the United States where religious freedom is held so dear? It has been claimed that a Gallup Poll conducted in 1989 for the Princeton Religious Research Centre, found that 82% of Americans believe that God created humans. Are these same people going to abandon their religious convictions at the urging of the U.N.? Such an idea is inconceivable. Nevertheless, to the Witness mind this is a realistic scenario and makes the preaching work more urgent as souls need to be saved from the impending disaster.

Identifying the true religion

The book *Mankind's Search for God* published by the Watchtower Society in 1990 lists ten identifying marks of the true religion.[5] Let us evaluate them individually:

1. The true religion worships the only true God, Jehovah.

On the surface this may seem like an obvious statement but there are a couple of points worth examining. Firstly the name of God. Most modern day translations of the Bible do not use the name "Jehovah" when referring to Almighty God. They use instead, titles such as Lord and Lord God. It is said that this can be traced back to an ancient Jewish superstition that held the personal name of God to be too sacred for mere humans to utter. With this in mind, the Jews for centuries substituted the word *Adonai* (Lord) or some other word whenever they came across the personal name of God in public reading.[6]

In modern times, beginning with William Tyndale's English translation in 1530, an attempt has been made by some to restore the original name. Unfortunately, only the consonants "YHWY" from the name have been preserved thus making the exact pronunciation unknown. The two most popular attempts are Yahweh and Jehovah.[7]

So the Witnesses are here saying that the true

religion must use God's name even though the correct pronunciation of that name is lost. Some have pointed out that if this was indeed as important to God as the Witnesses state, He would have preserved the correct pronunciation of the name for our use. Interesting too, is the fact that the name Jehovah does not appear at all in most New Testament translations, but can be found throughout the Witnesses' own Bible, the *New World Translation*.[8]

The Bible writers themselves do not always adhere to the Watchtower Society's insistence on the use of the Divine name. There are, in fact, entire letters written by the Apostles where the name "Jehovah" does not appear at all, even in the *New World Translation*. This is the case in Phillipians, First Timothy, Titus, Philemon, and the three letters of John.

There are also other "Sacred Name" movements that use the name "Jehovah" without any connection to the Watchtower Society. Clearly, simply using this name no more guarantees divine acceptance than do the names "Church of Christ" or "Assemblies of God." The second point of note is that this identifying mark precludes all non Christian religions. This may sit comfortably with the Western view of life but is likely to upset the 900 million Muslims, 700 million Hindus, 300 million Buddhists and 100 million adherents to Shinto to cite but a few examples.

2. The true religion offers access to God by means of Christ Jesus.

As far as most Christian religions are concerned

this would appear to be a central doctrine common to all. Offering prayer to God in Jesus' name seems to be the norm rather than the exception.

3. The true religion teaches and practices unselfish love.

Once again, rather than an identifying mark, this seems a basic tenet of all Christian faiths. The Witnesses will point out that many people professing to be Christian do not practice love of neighbour. This seems to my mind to be a comment on people rather than religion. To the extent that a religiously minded individual takes Jesus' example to heart, she will show love for others. This is true of all faiths including Jehovah's Witnesses.

One can legislate from the pulpit that the faithful should have love of neighbour but it is the individual that must practice it. Even among Jehovah's Witnesses we find evil deeds committed by the faithful. The Witnesses will point out that people are removed from the organisation if they are discovered engaging in "sin," but the fact remains that they were Witnesses at the time of their perceived sinful action.

4. The true religion remains untainted by worldly politics and conflicts. It is neutral in time of war.

Here is a statement that is certain to cause controversy. Whether an individual agrees that this should be true of religion or not will likely depend on their attitudes to issues such as nationalism, patriotism, world peace, war and political philosophy. It is true however that many mainstream religions have contributed toward, if not caused, wars and unrest over the years. It should be pointed out however that Jehovah's Witnesses are not the only religion to encourage conscientious objection during wartime.[9]

The entire issue of warfare and the involvement of Christians is a Gordian one. It is certainly true in the Old Testament that many faithful men served in the military. In the New Testament we have examples of military men such as the centurion of whom Jesus remarked:

"*I have not found anyone in Israel with such great faith*" (Matt. 8:10 NIV).

No reference by Jesus was made to his profession, nor was he required to change his vocation before Jesus granted the favour he requested.

The *Watchtower* itself in its issue of April 15 1903 put forward this direction:

"Obedience to the laws of the land might at some time oblige us to bear arms, and in such event it would be our duty to go into the army... There could be nothing against our *consciences* in going into the army"[10] (italics added)

The Watchtower issue of February 15 1951 indicated that the consciences of the Witnesses apparently now prohibited them from military service "It is only due to conscience that they have personally and legally objected before draft boards to participating in the armed conflicts and defense programs of worldly nations."[11]

This statement which contradicts the earlier one, and is now the official position of the Watchtower Society, seems to imply that the conscience of the *individual Witness* prevents each one from entering military service. The truth of the matter is however that any Witness entering the armed forces today would be disfellowshiped from the congregation and shunned by all.

5. The true religion lets God be true by accepting the Bible as God's Word.

Once again this may appear as a self evident fact. There is a subtext however. We could ask: Accepting the Bible in what fashion? In its historical and social context as a progressive revelation of truth, or as a 'flat surface upon which every text has equal value'.[12]

Although most Christian religions use the Bible as the basis for their belief, the Witnesses regard the Bible as inerrantly the word of God in every verse.[13] This means that the Bible stories of Adam and Eve, the flood of Noah's day and the consumption of Jonah by the mighty fish are to be taken as actual events. This presents enormous problems as we will see in the next chapter, but it is less of a distinguishing mark than the Witnesses themselves would like. In the United States alone, there are said to be tens of millions of "born again" Christians who subscribe to this same view of the Bible.

It is telling also that when a literal interpretation of the Bible's verses is so problematic as to stretch its credibility beyond all reason, the Witnesses are not averse to allowing a figurative interpretation. A good example of this exists with regard to the creative days of Genesis. We are told simply in the first book of the Bible that God's creative work progressed on a daily basis with mankind appearing on day six. The Bible even concludes each day with expressions such as

"And the evening and the morning were the fourth day."[14]

The Bible book of Exodus when discussing Israel's' obligation to honour the Sabbath uses the Genesis creative days as an example. Israel is told that God worked for six days and then rested on the seventh and in like manner they were to work for six days and then desist for the sabbath.[15] Obviously the reference in both cases was to twenty four hour days as we know them.

It was not until our modern day science revealed the great age of the earth and the life upon it that this account was seen to be flawed. At this time the Watchtower Society and others decided that the "days" of Genesis must refer to much longer periods of time. So much for the Bible being the inerrant word of God in every verse. It is in fact interesting to note that other fundamentalist groups that cling to the notion of twenty four hour creative days consider the witnesses' stand to be watering down the Bible message.

The Witnesses in fact seem to have their own rules for determining whether a Bible text should be taken literally or figuratively. This results in cases where parts of the *same verse* can interpreted differently. One example is the scripture found in Revelation chapter seven verse four:

"Then I heard the number of those who were sealed: 144,000 from all the tribes of Israel" (NIV).

The Watchtower Society holds that this number of 144,000 represents the precise number of faithful Christians that receive heavenly life. Therefore the number must be taken literally whereas the "tribes of

Israel" from whom these 144,000 are taken is to be understood symbolically as representing all mankind.[16] This kind of interpretation is simply a distortion of scripture to accommodate Watchtower theology. It seems that what is important is not what the Bible actually says, but what the Watchtower Society deem it to say. One is reminded of a character from another well known fantastical story:

"When I use a word,' Humpty Dumpty said, in rather a scornful tone, 'it means just what I choose it to mean — neither more nor less."

6. The true religion does not condone war or personal violence.

This seems to be a restatement of point four. I tend to think that the suspicions of most thinking people would be aroused by any religion that condoned personal violence.

7. The true religion successfully unites people of every race, language and tribe. It does not preach nationalism or hatred, but love.

Once again it would be a strange religion that preached hatred instead of love from the pulpit. Jehovah's Witnesses however, have made great strides in uniting their members across racial and nationalistic boundaries. This seems to be a process that is more successful in fundamental groups where the denomination's values are likely to be held more passionately by their members than some mainstream churches. This is not to say however that individuals from any church cannot cross the racial and linguistic barriers that divide mankind. Indeed much of the overseas work performed throughout different lands by relief agencies is done by religious organisations.

It should be noted also that the Witnesses are constantly presented with the achievements of their own organisation along these lines and are largely ignorant of the success of other religions. The Society's literature is employed in pointing out to the Witnesses all of the shortcomings within other organisations as if these simply did not exist within their own association. The truth is, of course, that within the Witness community we still find incidents of rape, child abuse, drug taking and alcoholism, suicide and murder. Reports are made (not in the Society's literature of course) of alcoholism and suicide even inside the international headquarters of the Jehovah's Witnesses' organisation.[17]

One could also ask whether the Witnesses are truly united or simply homogeneous because absolute conformity of thought and action is demanded of them.

8. The true religion advocates serving God, not for selfish gain or salary, but out of love. It does not glorify men. It glorifies God.

There are a couple of aspects here worthy of mention. It is true that Witness ministers are not paid a salary. Those who act as full time travelling overseers are supported by the congregations they visit, receiving food, board and expenses from the local church members.[18] Does this mean however, that a minister paid a salary by a congregation is any less worthy than one supported indirectly by the same congregation? To my mind this is just a question of the method used to support the minister as the principle remains the same.

The Witnesses will quickly point out the hierarchy of the large churches and the fancy garb that prominent ones wear. They perceive this to be giving glory to men and not God. On the other hand however, they will pay the airfare for a representative from the national branch committee to deliver a discourse at a local event of importance based, not on his ability as a speaker but his position within the organisation. This attitude of deference to senior Watchtower Society figures is seen time and again at large conventions where highly placed keynote speakers with the dullest of deliveries are used over more qualified but lowlier positioned ministers. It appears in this case that the Witnesses ought not to be casting the first stone.

Again it would seem logical to me that not the position, but the man occupying it is what ought to be scrutinised. Jesus' condemnation of the first century Pharisees comes to mind in this regard. Jesus in the Bible account did not attack the position these men occupied, but rather, the manner in which they discharged their responsibilities.

9. The true religion proclaims the Kingdom of God as man's sure hope, not some political or social philosophy.

Here is a requirement obviously tailored to reflect the unique doctrine of the Watchtower Society.

What then is the Kingdom of God? The Witnesses have a particular view of the Kingdom and see it as an actual government that will extend its rule from heaven over the entire earth in the near future.[19] Other religious commentators take a broader view allowing the Kingdom of God to be the rulership over all to which God has the inalienable right.[20] To submit to this Kingdom then, is to acknowledge this rulership and live the life of a Christian.

What the Witnesses are really saying therefore, is that the true religion must proclaim the Kingdom of God in the form that the Watchtower Society interprets it to be. It will come as no surprise that the Witnesses are alone in proclaiming the Kingdom in the fashion that they recognise it to exist. We are left with yet another circular argument. The true religion must have the correct understanding of God's Kingdom and the Witnesses have the true religion because they alone understand the real nature of that Kingdom. The Witnesses know that their understanding is correct because they have the true religion, and so on.

10. The true religion teaches the truth regarding God's purpose for man and the earth. It does not teach the religious lies of immortal soul and eternal torment in hell. It teaches that God is love.

Another circular argument. By whose standards do we determine what the truth regarding God's purpose for man and the earth actually is? Obviously each faith will have a belief regarding God's purpose and this will be promoted to those adhering to the faith as the true understanding.

The Witnesses will use the Bible to prove their own doctrines dealing with God's purpose for mankind but in the final analysis, it comes down to the interpretation that the Watchtower Society places on such scripture, and whether one accepts that the

Watchtower Society is led by God.

It is curious to note that the Witnesses' view of the mortality of the soul is not uniquely theirs, but is shared by the Seventh Day Adventists. This can be traced back to Russell's association with N.H. Barbour an Adventist minister.[21]

Obviously we can see from what we have considered so far that the Witnesses are anxious to distance themselves from the rest of the world's religions. They put much emphasis on proving the true faith from the false. These "ten identifying marks" are obviously carefully constructed to exclude all other faiths from the equation and highlight the Witnesses' exotic doctrinal interpretation. This practice is common in advertising where specific features of one product are compared to another.

The features that are compared in such advertisement are carefully selected to highlight the selling points of the advertised product. This would seem to be the Watchtower Society's tactic in this instance. Judged by their own criteria, the organisation shines in every respect. *Caveat emptor* would seem the order of the day in both instances.

To put this into context it should be kept in mind that the Witnesses imagine themselves and indeed all mankind to be involved in a great cosmic issue. The controversy revolves around the issue of who should rule mankind. They identify themselves with God on the one side and the Devil, aligned with all false religion, politics and commerce on the other. All of the suffering that mankind has endured down to our day is seen in the context of this struggle for supremacy.

Hence there are only two sides, and the Witnesses tend to focus very clearly on their own works and interpretations without having to weigh the views of any other organisation. They consider themselves and their society to be led directly by God and the only instrument employed by God to direct enlightenment into the world.

It is not surprising therefore that intolerance toward the doctrines and philosophies of other religions characterise their outlook.

The organisation's founders

A look at the men who gave the organisation its start will also be beneficial in determining whether this is the channel God has used to communicate his will to man. As we noted in chapter one, in the estimation of the Witnesses, Charles Russell occupied the unique position of being the one channel used by God to bring enlightenment to the world. The *Watchtower* magazine of March 1 1923 claimed of him:

"*Acting under the supervision* of the Lord, Brother Russell organised the *Watchtower Bible and Tract Society*"[22] (italics in original)

And again in the *Watchtower* magazine of September 15 1922:

"God gave Brother Russell the church to be as a mouthpiece for Him; and those who claim to have learned the truth apart from Brother Russell and his writings have been manifested by the Lord as deceivers, ready to lead the flock of God in their way."[23]

If this is true, and Charles Russell was the instrument used by God in re-establishing true worship in the earth, what would we expect from the teaching of one having the "truth"? Consider the following teachings from the one allegedly supervised by the Lord:

The Great Pyramid of Egypt.

For almost fifty years, from 1879 to 1928 the organisation taught that the Great Pyramid was an artefact of God's design, was to be studied by Christians, and held knowledge of future events locked into the riddle of its dimensions.

The book *Thy Kingdom Come (Studies in the Scriptures, vol III)* of 1881, has its tenth chapter entitled: "The testimony of God's stone witness and prophet, the Great Pyramid in Egypt." In this chapter we find the following words penned by Russell:

'Viewed from whatever standpoint we please, the Great Pyramid is certainly the most remarkable building in the world; but in the light of an investigation which has been in progress for the past thirty two years, it acquires new interest to every Christian advanced in the study of God's Word; for it seems in a remarkable manner to teach, in harmony with all the prophets, an outline of the plan of God, past, present and future.'[24]

The *Watchtower* of June 15 1922 attempted on page 187 to tie measurements of the Great Pyramid to Bible chronology with the following statement:

"In the passages of the Great Pyramid of Gizeh the agreement of one or two measurements with the present truth chronology might be accidental, but the corespondency of dozens of measurements proves that the same God designed both pyramid and plan - and at the same time proves the correctness of the chronology."[25]

Even more amazing than these strong statements regarding this "stone prophet" is the total reversal of this view in 1928 and the new position that in fact the Devil was behind the measurements of the pyramids all along!

The *Watchtower* of November 15 1928:

"If the pyramid is not mentioned in the Bible, then following its teachings is being led by vain philosophy and false science and not following after Christ."[26]

The same article went on to state:

"Then Satan put his knowledge in dead stone, which may be called Satan's Bible, and not God's stone witness. In erecting the pyramid, of course, Satan would put in it some truth, because that is his method of practising fraud and deceit."[27]

A total reversal. The same ancient construction is first proclaimed to be God's Witness and testimony to the accuracy of Watchtower Society chronology, and then vilified as a giant humbug and work of the Devil.

It is no surprise that the ancient Greeks listed the pyramids as one of the seven wonders of the world, nor that the pyramids are the only one of these wonders to survive to our modern day. It is also well known that the pyramids of Egypt have fascinated mankind for centuries and scholars have long searched for meanings behind their majesty.

But what can be said of these spiritual observations of long ago? Only one conclusion seems reasonable, they are not the teachings of God, communicated to Charles Russell but are merely the speculations of men of the time. It seems odd that if at this most crucial point in man's history, when according to the Witnesses, the true religion was being re-established in the earth, God would allow such a spurious teaching to be promoted by his "mouthpiece."

In the previously mentioned *Studies in the Scriptures vol III*, another equally bizarre claim can be found; that God resides on the star Alcyone in the Pleiades star system! We read:

"Alcyone, then, as far as science has been able to perceive, would seem to be 'the midnight throne' in which the whole system of gravitation has its seat, and from which the Almighty governs his universe..."[28]

This preposterous claim was accepted as truth for decades and in fact was expanded upon by Russell's successor nearly forty years later and was not contradicted until 1953.[29] Was this special insight into the location of Heaven itself personally communicated to Russell from God? If not, why was it permitted to be a teaching of the organisation God was said to be using?

The Leviathan of the Bible.

Many Bible commentators (including modern day

Witnesses) understand that the "Leviathan" spoken of in the book of Job chapters forty and forty one refers to the crocodile. The imagery of this powerful creature was used by the writer of the book of Job to contrast man and God and thereby demonstrate how feeble was man including Job himself.

Russell however, in his book *The Finished Mystery* (prepared and published posthumously by his successor J.F. Rutherford) relates this portion of scripture and adds comments in brackets to show the application in the modern day:

"*Thou wilt lengthen out Leviathan* [the locomotive] *with a hook* [automatic coupler] *or with a snare* [coupling pin] *which thou wilt cause his tongue* [coupling link] *to drop down. Wilt thou not place a ring* [piston] *in his nostrils* [cylinders] *or pierce through his cheeks* [piston ends] *with a staff* [piston rod]? *Will he make repeated supplication to thee* [to get off the track]? *Or will he utter soft tones unto thee* [when he screeches with the whistle]?"[30]

The account goes on to place the various parts of the steam locomotive into the Bible narrative.

This application to the steam locomotive may have had a glimmer of credibility when it was published in 1926 but did the steam locomotive so impress God that he gave this interpretation through his channel of communication on earth? Or rather, does it not simply represent the view of one man and his attempts to fit scripture into the context of his own generation? Certainly, if God was so impressed by the steam locomotive then he must be overawed by the space shuttle and the other splendid machines of our modern day.

As mentioned previously, more scandal was attached to Russell's name than many would consider appropriate for a "Man of God." The *Dictionary of American Biography* in its eighth edition makes the following observations regarding Russell:

"In 1909 his wife, Maria Frances Ackley, whom he had married in 1879, brought suit for divorce, alleging immoral conduct on Russell's part with female members of the church. The divorce was granted and though appealed five times by Russell was always sustained."[31]

The article continued: "In 1910 he travelled to Palestine... The next year he was in further trouble, owing to the sale in his church (at sixty dollars a bushel) of so-called "Miracle wheat" alleged to posses new and very marvellous agricultural properties; exposed by the *Brooklyn Daily Eagle*, he sued the paper for $100,000 damages in October 1911 but lost the case. In the midst of these difficulties he sailed away on a trip around the world, during which he devoted some time to a study of missionary work in the Orient."[32]

It should be noted that despite this scandal, and notwithstanding the imaginative nature of Russell's writings, the *Watchtower* magazine insisted on full conformity to Russell's teachings as if these were coming directly from God. In its March 1 1923 edition the *Watchtower* magazine commented:

"Every fellow servant has shown his ability or capacity and has increased the same in proportion as he has joyfully submitted to the Lord's will by working in the harvest field of the Lord in harmony with the Lord's way. Which way the Lord used Brother Russell to point out, because Brother Russell occupied the office of that "faithful and wise servant." He did the Lord's work according to the Lord's way. If, then Brother Russell did the Lords work in the lord's way, *any other way of doing it* is contrary to the Lord's way and therefore could not be a faithful looking after the interests of the Lord's kingdom."[33] (italics added)

It will remain for the reader to determine whether Russell acted "In the Lord's way."

A more detailed discussion of Russell and his exploits with the "miracle wheat" can be found in the book *Jehovah of the Watchtower* by Walter Martin and Norman Klann, published by Bethany House Publishers. This publication contains extracts from The *Brooklyn Daily Eagle*, the newspaper that exposed the scam as well as transcripts from the Russell vs Ross court case of 1913 in which Russell quite clearly committed perjury.

Upon his death in 1916, Russell was replaced by Joseph (Judge) Rutherford. Rutherford was a prolific writer and from most accounts took firm control of the organisation and was solely responsible for what was published in the *Watchtower* magazine.[34] This was highlighted in a dramatic way when four members of the board of directors sought to challenge and limit his authority. Rutherford had his helper A. H. Macmillan call a policeman who, with twirling nightstick, ejected four board members (a majority of the seven) from the Brooklyn headquarters.[35]

Macmillan later wrote a book entitled *Faith on the*

March and made this observation regarding Rutherford's style:

"Rutherford wanted to unify the preaching work and, instead of having each individual give his own opinion and tell what he thought was right and do what was in his own mind, gradually Rutherford himself began to be the main spokesman for the organisation. That was the way he thought the message could best be given without contradiction."[36]

It was during the presidency of these two men and later under Fredrick Franz that a pattern was set that seems to persist today in the minds of the Witnesses, namely, that an organisation of men (and in reality often one man)[37] can be relied upon to interpret the Bible account and that it is an act of disloyalty to God to differ from that interpretation even when it intrudes into private areas of life or has little actual support from the scriptures. Once this attitude takes root in the mind of a Witness, it is almost impossible for them to see beyond the revelations of the Watchtower Society.

It is an interesting fact that the Witnesses in general remain unperturbed by the failings and peccadillos of their society's founders. Whenever the discussion turns to such matters they are wont to quote the Bible book of Proverbs chapter four and verse eighteen which states:

"*But the path of the righteous ones is like the bright light that is getting lighter and lighter until the day is firmly established.*" (NWT)

The Watchtower Society contends that what this scripture reveals is that a steady process of spiritual illumination takes place among God's people, and therefore the fact that the founding fathers of the movement were often wrong in their understanding simply reflects the fact that they didn't have as much of the "light" from God as do the modern Governing Body. Essentially this means that whatever constitutes the "present truth" must be accepted by all Witnesses. The obvious questions that remain hanging in the air from this interpretation are "how do we know we now have *all* the truth?" and "what if our *present* understanding is wrong because we don't have all the "light" on the subject?" Employing a scriptural interpretation such as this, the Watchtower Society can change its position at any time and simply appeal to "new light" as justification. This is exactly what happens. The irony is that most Witnesses will simply accommodate this adjustment without question.

Let us return to Proverbs chapter four and verse eighteen however. Does this scripture really have reference to the *understanding* of the "righteous one"? The context of this verse demonstrates that it is the *way of life* (the path) of the "righteous one" which is being spoken of and not progressive prophetic revelations as the Watchtower Society would have us believe.

The "way" of the "righteous one" is contrasted in chapter four of Proverbs with the way or path of the "wicked" which leads to problems and hardships.[38] Obviously the reference is to the way of life or course of action that an individual chooses; the "righteous one" by virtue of his goodness does not stumble, his path is clear and bright. The "wicked," on the other hand, stumble around in darkness and bring trouble and strife upon themselves.

This is not a new or little known understanding of this Bible verse. Matthew Henry, Presbyterian Minister at Chester in Britain from 1687 to 1712, famous for his *Exposition of the Old and New Testaments*, makes the following comments on this verse:

"Their way shines to themselves in the joy and comfort of it: it shines before others in the lustre and honour of it; *it shines before men who see their good works,* ... *he that has clean hands shall be stronger and stronger.*"[39] (italics in original)

In speaking of "clean hands" and "good works" Matthew Henry obviously made the application of this verse to an individual's life course. Although his writings as well as others were available to the Watchtower Society throughout its history, it is not entirely surprising that the Society imbued this verse with its own special meaning considering the scant regard that it has shown to traditional religious scholars.

Beliefs of the Witnesses

To conclude this discussion and for those who may be interested, the following is a list of the main doctrines of the Watchtower Society condensed from their 1993 publication *Jehovah's Witnesses, Proclaimers of God's Kingdom.*[40]

The Bible is God's inspired Word. (2 Tim. 3:16,17)

What it contains is nor mere history or human

opinion but the word of God, recorded to benefit us.

Jehovah is the only true God. (ps. 83:18; Deut. 4:39)

Jehovah is the creator of all things, and as such, he alone deserves to be worshiped. Jehovah is the Universal Sovereign, the one to whom we owe full obedience.

Jesus Christ is the only-begotten Son of God, the only one created directly by God himself. (1 John 4:9, Col. 1:13-16)

Jesus was the first of God's creations; thus, before he was conceived and born as a human, Jesus lived in heaven. Jesus worships his Father as the only true God; Jesus never claimed equality with God. Jesus gave his perfect human life as a ransom for humankind. His sacrifice makes possible everlasting life for all who truly exercise faith in it. Jesus was raised from the dead as an immortal spirit person. Jesus has returned (having directed his attention as King toward the earth) and is now present as a glorious spirit.

Satan is the invisible "ruler of this world." (john 12:31. 1 John 5:19)

Originally he was a perfect son of God, but he allowed feelings of self-importance to develop in his heart, craved worship that belonged only to Jehovah, and enticed Adam and Eve to obey him rather than listen to God. Thus he made himself Satan, which means "Adversary." Satan "is misleading the entire inhabited earth"; he and his demons are responsible for increased distress on the earth in this time of the end. At God's appointed time, Satan and his demons will be destroyed forever.

God's Kingdom under Christ will replace all human governments and will become the one government over all humankind. (Dan. 7:13,14)

The present wicked system of things will be completely destroyed. The Kingdom of God will rule with righteousness and will bring real peace to its subjects. Wicked ones will be cut off forever, and worshipers of Jehovah will enjoy lasting security.

We are living now, since 1914, in "the time of the end" of this wicked world. (Matt. 24:3-14; 2 Tim. 3:1-5; Dan. 12:4)

During this time period, a witness is being given to all nations; after that will come the end, not of the globe, but of the wicked system of ungodly people.

There is only one road to life; not all religions or religious practices are approved by God. (Matt. 7:13,14; John 4:23,24; Eph. 4:4,5)

True worship emphasises not ritual and outward show but genuine love for God, shown by obedience to his commandments and by love for one's fellowman. People out of all nations, races, and language groups can serve Jehovah and have his approval. Prayer is to be directed only to Jehovah through Jesus; images are not to be used either as objects of devotion or as aids in worship. Spiritistic practices must be shunned. There is no clergy-laity distinction among true Christians. True Christianity does not include keeping a weekly sabbath or conforming to other requirements of the Mosaic Law in order to gain salvation; doing so would be a rejection of Christ, who fulfilled the Law. Those who practice true worship do not engage in interfaith. All who are truly disciples of Jesus get baptised by complete immersion. All who follow Jesus' example and obey his commandments bear witness to others about the Kingdom of God.

Death is a result of inheritance of sin from Adam. (Rom. 5:12; 6:23)

At death, it is the soul itself that dies. The dead are conscious of nothing. Hell (Sheol, Hades) is mankind's common grave. The "lake of fire" to which the incorrigibly wicked are consigned signifies, as the Bible itself says, "second death," death forever. Resurrection is the hope for the dead and for those who have lost loved ones in death. Death due to Adamic sin will be no more.

A "little flock" of only 144,000, go to heaven. (Luke 12:32; Rev. 14:1,3)

These are the ones who are "born again" as spiritual sons of God. God selects these ones out of all peoples and nations to rule as kings with Christ in the Kingdom.

Others who have God's approval will live forever on earth. (Ps. 37:29; Matt. 5:5; 2 Pet. 3:13)

Earth will never be destroyed or depopulated. In harmony with God's original purpose, all the earth will become a paradise. There will suitable homes and an abundance of food for everyone. Sickness, all kinds of disability, and death itself will become things of the past.

Secular authorities are to be treated with due respect. (Rom 13:1-7; Titus 3:1,2)

True Christians do not share in rebellion against governmental authority. They obey all laws that do not conflict with the law of God, but obedience to God comes first. They imitate Jesus in remaining neutral as to the world's political affairs.

Christians must conform to Bible standards regarding blood as well as sexual morality. (Acts 15:28,29)

Taking blood into the body through mouth or veins violates God's law. Christians are to be morally clean; fornication, adultery, and homosexuality must have no place in their lives, neither should drunkenness or drug abuse.

Personal honesty and faithfulness in caring for marital and family responsibilities are important for Christians. (2 Tim. 5:8; Col. 3:18-21; Heb. 13:4)

Dishonesty in speech or business, as well as playing the hypocrite, are not consistent with being a Christian

Acceptable worship of Jehovah requires that we love him above all else. (Luke 10:27; Deut. 5:9)

Doing Jehovah's will, thus bringing honour to his name, is the most important thing in the life of a true Christian. While doing good to all persons as they are able, Christians recognise a special obligation toward fellow servants of God; so their help in times of illness or disaster is directed especially toward these. Love of God requires of true Christians not only that they obey his commandment to love their neighbour but also that they not love the immoral and materialistic way of life of the world. True Christians are no part of the world and so refrain from joining in activities that would identify them as sharing its spirit.

The Trouble With Science

"Science, in other words knowledge, is not
the enemy of religion, for if so, then religion
would mean ignorance. But it is often the
antagonist of school-divinity."

Oliver Wendell Holmes

As discussed in the previous chapter, the
Witnesses regard everything in this world to be under
the control of the Devil. They consider the principal
aim of the Devil to be the eradication of true worship
from the earth by whatever means he has at his
disposal.[1]

In this context, any science or field of knowledge
that is at odds with the Watchtower Society's
interpretation of the Bible is condemned as the work
of the Devil. They are particularly concerned that the

literalness of the Bible is under attack from modern scientific discoveries. Nowhere is this more true than in the creation - evolution debate. The whole concept of evolution is seen by the Witnesses to be a God dishonouring work of darkness.

The scientific method is not the only field of human endeavour to come under suspicion however. The witnesses take every opportunity to point out in their literature the shortcomings of mankind as if somehow this will leave the wisdom of the Bible in stark contrast.[2] All fields of scientific endeavour come under scrutiny including medicine, physics, chemistry and engineering. This suspicion of "worldly" knowledge can become almost a paranoia and have a deep seated affect on the lives of some Witnesses as we will see in chapter nine.

In this chapter I will examine the creation - evolution debate and the problems that plague the Witnesses and other fundamentalists due to their literal interpretation of the book of Genesis.

The first eleven chapters of Genesis have come under intense scrutiny by religious and scientific minds for many hundreds of years. This section of the book of beginnings covers the foundation of the universe, the creation of life on earth including man and woman and man's subsequent fall from grace. The story traces the deterioration of society culminating in the Noachian flood and then the spread of mankind again concluding with the God - King Nimrod, the tower of Babel and the confusing of mankind's language. A great deal of time and history is compressed in to a very few words.

As we have said, the Witnesses take this section of scripture to be a factual and historically accurate account of life's beginnings and man's colonisation of the planet.

I will divide the account of Genesis into several sections and outline the problems introduced by a literal explication of the events described. I will also examine the book *Life - How did it get here? By evolution or by creation?* which is the most recent Watchtower Society text on the subject and in doing so I will unveil its intellectual dishonesty.

Beginnings

"In the beginning God created the heavens and the earth."

With this simple statement the Bible opens. Like so much of the first book of the Bible it is bereft of detail. A fact is stated, a scientific explanation is not given.

Many fundamentalist religious groups insist that this creation event can be dated from Bible chronology. In 1654 James Ussher the Anglican Archbishop of Armagh, Ireland calculated that creation began on Saturday October 22 4004 BC.[3] Others that hold to a literal interpretation of Genesis (Creation Scientists etc.) allow the Earth and the universe to be no older than about 10,000 years.[4] This obviously conflicts with the deductions of the scientific community which put the age of the universe at approximately 14 billion years and the earth at 4.5 billion years.

It is an interesting feature of the Witnesses' literature that they are not troubled as are some other groups by the great ages that science attaches to the earth itself. They regard the first sentence of Genesis as stating a fact concerning the universe that chronologically precedes the creation account of life on the planet.[5] In taking this view they avoid the hoop-jumping required to explain away the mountain of evidence testifying against a young earth. It is interesting that for this "lapse of faith" they are criticised by other fundamentalist movements.

Chapter one of Genesis deals with God's creative works, these being accomplished in periods of time referred to as "days." Before the nineteenth century, these were taken to be literal twenty four hour days as we know them. After all, it was reasoned, could not the almighty create the cosmos in only a few hours or even in an instant of time if he wished? During the nineteenth century however, it became increasingly obvious that the earth and life upon it was indeed very old and that some life forms preceded others by time periods far in excess of one day.

This led many Bible scholars to the conclusion that the "days" of Genesis were symbolic and represented much longer and unspecified time periods. The Witnesses adopted a position similar to this but for reasons which make little sense fixed on a period of 7000 years as the length of a creative day. In more recent times they have attempted to soften this absurd chronology by stating that the days were in fact thousands of years long without reference to the earlier stated 7000 year period.[6] Of course, in the context of evolutionary time, 7,000 years is simply a heartbeat.

The order of the creative "days" has also been the subject of much controversy. For example vegetation was created on the third day whereas the sun did not appear until the fourth. Insects which play a vital role in the pollination of plants were not created until the fifth day. This suggests that plants survived for thousands of years without light and still longer without insects.

To question this discrepancy is simply to betray a lack of faith according to the Watchtower Society as the following quotation demonstrates:

"Why should we doubt that the One who created the vegetation in all its amazing diversity could also see to it that, before the appearance of insects, the plants were pollinated in one of the above ways (wind or water etc.) or in still other ways that men have not discovered?"[7]

This tactic of invoking divine intervention when things become difficult characterises the Witnesses' excursions into the scientific arena. It was summed up well by Isaac Asimov when he said:

"However much the creationist leaders might hammer away at their "scientific" and "philosophical" points, they would be helpless and a laughing stock if that were all they had. It is religion that recruits their squadrons. Tens of millions of Americans, who neither know nor understand the actual arguments for - or even against - evolution, march in the army of the night with their Bibles held high. And they are a strong and frightening force, impervious to, and immunised against, the feeble lance of mere reason."[8]

Ignoring the abovementioned day-order discrepancy, the Witnesses' creation book postulates a ten stage process loosely based on the Genesis account of creation and then makes the sweeping statement that:

"Science agrees that these stages occurred in this general order."[9]

Although by just one example we have seen that this is not the case, the Witnesses forge ahead and use the science of probability to calculate the likelihood of the author of Genesis arriving at these ten steps without divine revelation. This process defies logic and will appeal only to those who have already suspended their critical thinking or who bring to the discussion a prior belief in the historicity of Genesis.

The garden of Eden

In chapters two and three of Genesis God's creative work is climaxed by the appearance of man and woman (it is generally recognised that there are in fact two creation accounts in the book of Genesis). This glory is short lived however as both fall from grace after only the briefest honeymoon together. I will discuss the issues of morality and justice raised by this episode in the next chapter.

The man is placed in the garden of Eden and his God-given work is to tend and cultivate it. At this point a prohibition is laid upon the man that he must not eat from a specific tree referred to as "the tree of the knowledge of good and evil." The punishment for breaking this law is death. This notion of a forbidden action is a recurring theme in folklore and is often used to explain the presence of evil. In the Greek myths for example, the first woman Pandora is given a box by the Gods and warned not to open it. She of course does and all the ills of mankind are released.

After naming all of the animals in the garden, it becomes obvious to the first man that although animal life exists in pairs, he is alone. God perceives this state of affairs to be undesirable and so determines to make a companion for Adam. Accordingly, God takes a rib from the man and clones, not another man, but a "wife-man" or woman. Thus the account sets the scene for male dominance to persist for thousands of years. The female is obviously subsidiary to the man being created second and only then from a rib of the man himself. Furthermore the fact that the man names the woman as he did with the animals indicates his dominion over her.

Scientifically, it could be argued that the female is in fact the more important with the male being a mere adjunct. It is the female among mammals that supplies the initial environment for the development of the young. Females are also better at surviving stress and tend to have a life span some six or seven years longer than males. The writer of Genesis, however, was not to know this and instead reflected his cultural outlook.

Adam's joy at receiving his new mate proves to be fleeting as a third and more sinister character emerges in the account. We are told that the snake was more "crafty"[10] than the other beasts of the field. This may indeed have appeared to be the case to the writer of Genesis. Snakes seem to be crafty inasmuch as they move silently and can attack before being seen. In fact a snake is a reptile and as such is generally less intelligent than a mammal but for the sake of the narrative its mystery served it well.

The snake now converses with the woman and challenges what God has said regarding the "tree of the knowledge of good and evil." The woman (who apparently is nonchalant at being accosted by a talking reptile) recounts to the snake God's prohibition concerning the tree and actually embellishes it by saying that just to touch the fruit would spell death. The snake then directly contradicts this and convinces the woman to eat, after which she gives some to her husband and he eats also. The two then realise their nakedness and manufacture loincloths to cover themselves.

When God discovers their sin (only after calling to them, as they were hiding in fear) he pronounces sentence upon them all (snake included). For the man there is to be hardships in tilling the ground as a farmer. The women is condemned to painful childbirth and domination by her husband (thus guaranteeing centuries of oppression), for her special and greater guilt in being the first to yield to temptation. The snake is sentenced to eat dust and go upon its belly.

A snake, of course, does not eat dust but to the uninformed writer of Genesis it may have appeared that the constant flicking of the tongue near the ground served to lick up dust. Modern science has now revealed that the heat sensitive tongue of the snake is used to detect subtle chemical information in the air as it seeks out its prey.[11]

In order that the disgraced couple might not gain entrance to the "tree of life" and thus live forever, they are evicted from the garden. We are here presented with an odd depiction of a God that can ostensibly be overridden by one of his creatures. The suggestion is that Adam really could have lived forever if he gained access to the "tree of life" and God would have been helpless to stop him. This view of God seems more in keeping with the Gods of Homer's epics who are given to human failings.

To ensure that no humans in the future would be able to raid the "tree of life" and presumably thereby live forever, guards, in the form of cherubs with a flaming sword are placed on the path to the tree.

The flood

It is evident from the Genesis account that mankind went from bad to worse. The narrative tells us that the whole earth was "filled with violence"[12] and therefore God decreed that a destruction must take place. The only individuals worth saving in the estimation of God are Noah and his wife, Noah's three sons and their wives. The method of survival is to be by means of a large boat the dimensions of which are given to Noah.

As everyone knows, Noah was instructed to take into the ark two of each kind of living thing (actually seven of the "clean" beasts) to ensure their preservation. It is an interesting aside to note that the distinction between "clean" and "unclean" animals which denotes their suitability for sacrifice was not explained until the book of Leviticus, much later in the Bible. One can only speculate that Noah must have received the criteria for distinguishing the two directly from God.

The story concludes with the flood waters annihilating life from the planet, then subsiding followed by the release of all the animals which presumably spread out and repopulated the globe. Unfortunately in my view, the Witnesses insist that these events actually took place on a global scale, and that all life outside the ark did indeed perish, with the entire planet being deluged. It is my contention that no reasonable person should be asked to believe this. I will look at just some of the difficulties this literal view creates from a scientific perspective as I believe that the attempt to justify this story as an historical occurrence does much to undermine the credibility afforded to other parts of the Bible by people in general.

How big was the ark?

Genesis 6:15: "And this is how you should make it: the length of the ark three hundred cubits, its breadth fifty cubits, and its height thirty cubits." (NAB)

The Watchtower Society calculates from these Bible measurements that the usable capacity of the ark was approximately 1,300,000 cubic feet[13] and asserts that this is equal to the capacity of ten freight trains of forty eight American stock cars each. This certainly sounds impressive and indeed to the ancient writers of the Genesis account such a capacious vessel would have appeared more than adequate for the task. Bear in mind that the Bible writers likely identified not more than a few hundred different animals in total.

We are not told how four carpenters, presumably inexperienced at ship building, managed to construct such a vessel, or how a wooden structure approximately 450 feet long and only seventy five feet wide could withstand the huge torsional stress that would be placed upon it. There was certainly no tradition of ship building on the scale of the ark at that time in human history, and since that time there has never been a wooden ship built with the length of the ark as specified in the Bible.

Where did the water come from?

Genesis 7:11: "In the six hundredth year of Noah's life, in the second month, on the seventeenth day of the month, on the same day all the fountains of the great deep burst open, and the flood gates of the sky were opened." (NAB)

In talking about the "fountains of the great deep" the Bible seems to indicate that not only rain was involved but perhaps tidal wave action also. The Watchtower Society insists that prior to the flood, a giant water canopy existed over the earth through which the sun shone hazily.[14] It was this water canopy, say the Witnesses, that collapsed upon the hapless population and deluged the earth. This is an old notion and was proposed in 1874 by a Quaker Bible scientist named Isaac Newton Vail.[15] There are many difficulties with this scenario.

Firstly the Genesis account tells us that the flood waters encompassed the entire earth, covering the highest mountains including, one presumes, Mount Everest at 29,028 feet. The Watchtower Society argues that the mountains were much lower in the days of Noah and were raised to their present height by the pressure of the flood water, but no real evidence exists to support this view. To cover mountains such as Everest requires an enormous quantity of water. It has been estimated that 4,400,000,000 cubic kilometers of water would be necessary if the highest mountains were to be submerged.[16] This much water suspended above the earth in a water canopy would result in an atmospheric pressure hundreds of times greater than at present and certainly more than the pre-flood creatures of earth could have endured.

Secondly, it has also been estimated, that from a thermodynamic perspective, this quantity of water falling as rain would have raised the temperature of the earth to such an extent that the oceans would have boiled.[17] For each kilogram of water condensed from the atmosphere 2.26 million joules of energy must be given up as heat. The effect of liberating the required amount of water to flood the earth would raise the temperature of the atmosphere in excess of 3500 degrees centigrade during the time of the flood. Of course, the ancient writers of the Bible knew nothing of thermodynamics.

Finally, even if we disregard the first two problems, the question remains, where did all the water go? While it is true that our earth really is a "water planet" with oceans covering more than 70% of its surface, the total volume of water in existence today has been computed to be 1,370,000,000 cubic kilometres,[18] which is less than a third of the volume needed to cover the highest mountains. From these few examples it should be obvious that the flood of the Bible was at most a local phenomenon limited to the relatively flat area of the Tigris-Euphrates valley.

What did the ark contain?

As stated earlier, the Bible depicts animals entering principally by twos. With the limited knowledge possessed by the Bible writers, it may have seemed reasonable that a single pair was sufficient for survival. Modern science however reveals a different picture with considerable research having been conducted into threatened populations. Today the likelihood of repopulation from the survival of a single pair of animals would be very slender considering the tiny gene-pool from which to draw as well as numerous other difficulties.

The Watchtower Society attempts to minimise the difficulties involved in shoehorning all of earth's creatures into a single vessel with statements such as:

"Also, investigation reveals that, of some 3,000 'species' of land mammals classified by zoologists, only about 300 include any that are larger than a horse, whereas some 2,200 are no larger than a rabbit. Marine mammals such as the huge whales and dolphins would be no problem, as they would have remained outside the ark."[19]

This does not really help their cause at all as even if Noah's assignment was to save these mammals only, the ark would still have been too small. Remember that these animals had to be fed for a whole year until the flood waters subsided. Using the Society's own calculations, the capacity of 480 railway box cars does not appear to be much when food to last a year for over 300 pairs of animals larger than a horse must be carried as well as over two thousand pairs of smaller creatures together with Noah and his family and their provisions.

Elephants alone can consume up to 225kg of grasses and leaves per day as well as 190 litres of water. Even if we allow their restricted movement within the ark to take the edge of their appetite somewhat, Noah would still have needed over 80 tonnes of food and almost 70,000 litres of water to satisfy his pair of elephants during their year long voyage, and this at half rations.

This of course ignores the 8,500 species of birds, 2,500 species of snakes, 3,000 species of lizards, 3,100 species of amphibians, and so on, not to mention the nearly one million species of insects that have been classified, a figure which is said to be only one third of the actual number in existence. Nor do Noah's instructions allow for marine creatures which are inherently sensitive to small changes in sea temperature or salinity. One can well imagine the effect on such marine life when trillions of gallons of freshwater are dumped into their habitat. The account also makes no mention of land plants. These would be just as dead after twelve months under water as the rest of life outside the ark.

It would also have been quite a task loading these animals into the ark. The Bible tells us that all of the ark's inhabitants boarded in one day. If we allow fifteen hours of daylight, then just to load the mammals, reptiles, birds, and amphibians would require one pair of animals to embark every 2.7 seconds. This doesn't give those inside the ark much time to lead each pair to its pen and settle them down. One is left to speculate on how Noah managed to house the 2,000 species of termites on his wooden vessel, or how he managed to stop them breeding aboard the ark with some species able to lay 30,000 eggs in a single day.

If then, the words of Genesis are to be taken literally, the ark must have contained anywhere from two to four million animals with up to four fifths of them being insects. Clearly to cram all of these onto a primitive wooden boat and keep them alive for twelve months is absurd. The Watchtower Society however, muddy the waters by appealing to the Genesis description of created "kinds."[20] The account tells us that the animals went into the ark according to "their kinds."

Although the Genesis "kind" is a moving target, the Watchtower Society infers that all of the members of the Felis genus, for example, including the mountain lion and the housecat, were derived from the two archetypal cats preserved on the ark.[21] To say that all species extant today developed from fundamental "kinds" over a time span of little more than 4,000 years is to postulate evolution on a scale that would make even the most avowed evolutionist sceptical.

The question of the creature's dispersal after the flood is also left unanswered. For example, how did koalas and platypuses find their way back to Australia? If one assumes that animals naturally spread out from the ark, said to be located somewhere in Turkey, why is it that the fossil remains of many of Australia's unique wildlife are found only in Australia? How did Australia's marsupials make it back home with their continent surrounded by oceans? The same is true of Central and South America. Here we find in the fossil record evidence of distinctive groups found only in these areas such as rat possums, fossil opossums, New World monkeys, marmosets, as well as many unique birds and reptiles. Why, if animals spread out gradually from the ark after the flood, do we not find these fossils anywhere else?

Finally, not only was the ark crammed to the gunwales with animals, birds, reptiles, insects and the like, all of the known parasitical organisms must have been present, because to argue that these have evolved since the flood is once again to accelerate the process to a tempo which even evolutionists would not sanction. And what of the diseases that affect humans, many of which have been known for thousands of years? Noah and his family would have been carrying such things as leprosy, measles, poliomyelitis, typhus, malaria, gonorrhea, syphilis, smallpox, typhoid fever and the like. Add to this the poor sanitation that would have attended such a primitive vessel and one begins to wonder how any of them survived. Obviously to accept such nonsense, faith rather than common sense is the order of the day.

If, in the final analysis, an appeal must be made to

divine intervention or miracle to overcome these difficulties, why is the account presented as being scientifically sound in the first instance? If it is to be a matter of faith, then let it be so, but let us have no more of this pseudo-scientific foolishness.

The creation book

As I have mentioned previously, the principle textbook of the Watchtower Society on the analysis of evolution is the book *Life - How did it get here? By evolution or by creation?* first published in 1985 and commonly known in the Witness community as the "creation" book.

When this book was first announced, I can clearly remember the speaker at the convention where the publication was to be released endorsing it with the statement:

"If anyone still believes in evolution after reading this book, then he must want to."

Although uncomfortable with this classic fundamentalist conceit, I was anxious to examine the publication due to my interest in the entire debate. It came as a disappointment however to discover the same mixture of logical fallacy, circular reasoning, ad hominem attacks and provincialism that had typified previous excursions into the area. What concerned me even more, however, was the misleading use of references to support Watchtower Society argumentation.

Within this publication, quotations are taken out

of context or used in a way that clearly misrepresents what the author was trying to convey. This intellectual dishonesty cannot be justified by an all's-fair-in-love-and-war attitude simply because the evolutionary theory is perceived to be the Devil's work. Scholastic sloppiness of this sort merely undermines the credibility of the work (of which it has precious little to begin with) and serves only to convince those who know no better.

Obviously it is beyond the scope of this chapter to present a detailed examination of the evidence presented for and against evolution, and so I will confine my consideration to the *methods* used by the Watchtower Society in attacking the scientific perspective.

Credentials

A quick glance through the listing of the reference material at the rear of the creation book demonstrates the superficial nature of the publication. The first eight chapters of the work introduce the evidence against evolution and cite no less than 242 references in support of that evidence. Of these 242 however, 65 are references to newspaper articles or magazines, at least 27 refer to scientists whose disciplines lie outside of the debate such as astronomers Carl Sagan and Fred Hoyle. 10 more refer to the Time-Life series of books published in the early sixties aimed at the home market, and so the list goes on.

Intellectual dishonesty

To demonstrate the publication's scant regard for the intent of those it quotes I will examine a number of references and compare them with the original material.

The Watchtower Society is fond of quoting Frances Hitching's publication *The Neck of the Giraffe* and uses his material thirteen times in the first eight chapters of the creation book. It should be borne in mind that although the Society describe Hitching as an "evolutionist" when introducing his first quotation, he is not a respected authority on the topic, and indeed, has come under severe criticism for his treatment of the subject.

Richard Dawkins, the respected zoologist, in his book *The Blind Watchmaker* comments on Hitching's work, noting that it contained:

"A very large number of errors which would quickly have been spotted if an unemployed biology graduate, or indeed an undergraduate, had been asked to glance through the manuscript."[22]

I suspect however, that even Hitching would be less than pleased with the manner in which his work is presented by the Watchtower Society. Hitching is first quoted in chapter two of the creation book to support the Society's assertion that the theory of evolution is not an established fact and is subject to disagreement among scientists.

It is here that we also see a subtle artifice emerging. The Watchtower Society attempts to constitute Darwinism and evolution as equal in the mind of the reader. This is done by both misrepresenting the true position of those whose work is quoted, and by replacing terms such as "natural selection," "Darwinism" and "Neo-Darwinism" with "evolution" or "the modern day theory of evolution." Some may argue that this is done for the sake of readability but this excuse is unacceptable to my mind as the outcome is to convey the impression that evolutionists are in doubt about evolution itself. This is clearly the objective of the chapter.

As an example of the first tactic mentioned, that of misrepresenting the author's real position, let us return to the Society's first quotation from Hitching's work:

"Frances Hitching, an evolutionist and author of the book The Neck of the Giraffe, stated: "For all its acceptance in the scientific world as the great unifying principle of biology, Darwinism, after a century and a quarter, is in a surprising amount of trouble.""[23]

The quotation from Hitching's book is accurate, it is the context in which it is used that makes it deceptive. The chapter heading in the creation book is "Disagreements About Evolution-Why?" and the Subheading under which the quote appears is "Evolution Under Assault." To the general public this initiates the impression (deliberately I'm sure) that Darwinism (a method for explaining the mechanism of evolution) and the fact of evolution itself are one and the same.

That this is not the case in Hitching's mind is evident from the very next paragraph following the Society's quote:

"Evolution and Darwinism are often taken to mean the same thing. But they don't. Evolution of life over a very long period of time is a fact, if we are to believe evidence gathered during the last two centuries from Geology, paleontology (the study of fossils), molecular biology and many other scientific disciplines. Despite the many believers in Divine creation who dispute this (including about half the adult population of the United States, according to some opinion polls), *the probability that evolution has occurred approaches certainty in scientific terms.*"[24] (italics added)

So clearly, Hitching himself does not question the process of evolution, although one could be forgiven for believing that he does after reading extracts from his work published in the creation book.

To further ensure that the unsuspecting readers of the creation book remain confused on this point, subsequent extracts from Hitching's work evade the term "Darwinism" and in one instance where it is unavoidable, substitute the term "the modern evolution theory"[25] Either the Watchtower Society's researchers are incompetent (possible but unlikely) or have no regard for the truth in their attempt to squash this scientific viewpoint which remains at odds with their own doctrinal position.

Even Darwin himself is not immune from this word substitution ploy. The creation book quotes Darwin in The Origin of Species as saying:

"To suppose that the eye... could have been formed by [evolution], seems, I freely confess, absurd in the highest degree."[26]

The word "evolution" in brackets actually replaces the term "natural selection" in the original text.[27] The Watchtower Society may see this substitution as a trivial point, but to my mind it is a cynical ploy to lead the reader's mind into accepting that all argument regarding evolutionary method and process serve to undermine the concept of evolution.

As with the quote from *The Neck of the Giraffe*, this extract from The Origin of Species does not tell the whole story. One could be forgiven, after reading Darwin's quote in the creation book, for thinking that Darwin himself found absurd the notion of complex organs arising from natural selection. That this was not the case, is obvious from Darwin's statement only a few paragraphs further:

"If it could be demonstrated that any complex organ existed, which could not possibly have been formed by numerous, successive, slight modifications, my theory would break down. *But I can find no such case.*"[28] (italics added)

A reading in context of the quotation used by the Watchtower Society from The Origin of Species reveals that Darwin is saying that, while acknowledging that the formation of complex organs (such as the eye) might seem unlikely at first, this personal incredulity must not be permitted to overshadow one's reasoning and thus blind one to the possibility that natural selection was in fact responsible. Clearly, in both examples tendered, the real position of the author has been misrepresented.

The fossil record

The Watchtower Society dismiss all evidence for evolution from the fossil record by recourse to various tactics. They are particularly scornful of the fossilised transitional form Archaeopteryx, discovered in limestone rock in Bavaria and possessing both reptilian and avian characteristics. Notice the subtle implication in this extract from the creation book:

"At one time evolutionists believed that Archaeopteryx, meaning "ancient wing" or "ancient bird," was a link between reptile and bird. But now, many do not. Its fossilised remains reveal perfectly formed feathers on aerodynamically designed wings capable of flight. Its wing and leg bones were thin and hollow. Its supposed reptilian features are found in birds today. And it does not predate birds, because fossils of other birds have been found in rocks of the same period as Archaeopteryx."[29]

The subtext is obviously that evolutionists no longer believe Archaeopteryx to be a genuine transitional link between reptiles and birds, that somehow it has been discredited, that it is just another species of extinct bird. This is simply not true.

Archaeopteryx is classified as a bird due to one characteristic - feathers. Its "supposed" reptilian features found in other birds (some extinct) are claws and teeth. But as is often the case, we have not been told the whole story by the Watchtower Society. Archaeopteryx is distinguishable as an intermediate between reptiles and birds because it also has a long series of tail vertebrae, unfused back vertebrae, unfused limb bones, rudimentary breastbone, solid limb bones etc.[30] All of these characteristics are possessed by other small reptiles found at the same time.[31]

As for debate in the scientific community over the validity of Archaeopteryx as an intermediate form, consider the words of Associate Professor Michael Archer of the NSW School of Zoology:

"It would be difficult to imagine a more perfect link. If there has been any significant debate among paleontologists about the evolutionary significance of Archaeopteryx, it is not about its intermediate position between birds and reptiles but rather about the particular group of reptiles to which it is most closely related."[32]

It would appear that, far from dismissing Archaeopteryx as a transitional form, the scientific community is united in its acceptance of this "link."

The Watchtower Society's claim that fossilised birds have also be found in rocks of the same period as Archaeopteryx is also a dubious one. The supporting reference in the creation book for this statement is Francis Hitching's book *The Neck of the Giraffe*, however here the trail stops as Hitching quotes Yale paleontologist John Ostrom without giving us the source and thus we are unable to verify the claim.

What is of interest is that the Ostrom quote is said by Hitching to be from 1977. Stephen Jay Gould in his book The Panda's Thumb, published in 1983, discusses the work that Ostrom has done with the five Archaeopteryx skeletons:

"Yale paleontologist John Ostrom... restudied every specimen of Archaeopteryx - all five of them... Ostrom documents in impressive detail the extreme similarity in structure between Archaeopteryx and coelurosaurs."[33]

It would appear that this scientist does not doubt the authenticity of Archaeopteryx as an intermediate form, his work has actually strengthened its position as ancestral to modern birds. Once again we have been treated to a very superficial and one sided presentation of the evidence. The Watchtower Society in its haste to bolster its own position demonstrates its intellectual dishonesty by misleading its followers with selective quotations and inference.

Dating

As we have already seen, the Watchtower Society allows the creative days of Genesis to represent periods of time which may be "millenniums" in length. Even if we revert to the previously mentioned figure of 7,000 years for each Genesis "day," as aquatic life was not created until day five in the Bible account and terrestrial life appeared on day six, the oldest marine life therefore can have existed for only 20,000 years, the oldest land animals for 13,000 years and man's own history stretches back a mere 6,000 years.

As a consequence of this "day-age" interpretation of Genesis, the enormous ages claimed by science for the fossil record causes the Watchtower Society much difficulty. The Society's solution to this inconvenience is simply to dismiss the dating methods used by modern science as hopelessly inaccurate. The creation book is used by the Society as its front-line weapon in this regard.

The only method of dating that receives any real attention in the creation book is radiocarbon dating, and this is claimed to be unreliable for objects prior to 2,000 BC.[34] Given the Society's predilection for deceptive argument, one may ask, is this all there is to the story? Is this even the real position? The fact is that the dating of rocks by radioactive decay underpins activities such as mineral and petroleum exploration.[35] If the method was as unreliable as the Watchtower Society would like us to believe, would commercial oil companies be likely to spend money using the technique? A fact not mentioned by the creation book is that in addition to dating methods that analyse Carbon 14, there are other methods involving Uranium 238, Uranium 235, Thorium 232, Potassium 40, Rubidium 87, as well as techniques which do not rely on radioactivity at all.

A vast and well established body of science stands in opposition to the chronology postulated by the Witnesses. The Watchtower Society dismisses this science all too quickly in its attempt to lead the minds of its followers to its own sectarian conclusion.

Early man

The Witnesses, in common with other Christian fundamentalist groups, find the concept of man's evolution from more primitive forms to be particularly offensive as the Bible portrays man as the zenith of God's creation. It will therefore come as no surprise that the chapter devoted to "ape men" in the creation book summarily dismisses any evidence for this scenario.

Typical of this dismissive attitude is the treatment meted out to the australopithecines and particularly the species aferensis, the best known of which is "Lucy" discovered in 1974 by Donald Johanson. After the usual selection of single sentence quotes, the creation book concludes the examination with the words:

"If any australopithecines were found alive today, they would be put in zoos with other apes. No one would call them "ape-men." The same is true of other fossil "cousins" that resemble it such as the smaller type of australopithecine called "Lucy"...Obviously it too was simply an "ape.""[36]

This process is characteristic of Watchtower Society publications, where the evidence against their case is presented and then dismissed as having no real validity. The non discerning reader is lulled into thinking that both sides of the argument have been presented with the weight of evidence falling, of course, on the side of the Watchtower Society. In fact, nothing could be farther from the truth.

In the case of the australopithecine "Lucy," consider the description given by Dr. C. Loring Brace, professor of anthropology at the Museum of Anthropology, University of Michigan:

"Brain size was approximately the same as that found in the large modern anthropoid apes. The crowns of the molar teeth had the same cusp and fissure pattern visible in the Miocene Dryopithecines and also in modern apes and humans. The canines however, did not project in a functional way beyond the occlusal level of the rest of the teeth. In this trait, the Australopithecines resembled human beings and differed from all other primates.

Finally, the spinal chord entered the skull at the bottom and not towards the back as in quadruped mammals, and this, confirmed later by discoveries of pelvic and lower limb bones, showed that the Australopithecines stood erect. In fact, careful anatomical and biomechanical studies have demonstrated that they were erect-walking bipeds whose mode of locomotion was not different from that of modern Homo sapiens (Lovejoy, Heiple and Buretein 1973). This is the cautious, checked, and tested conclusion of all of the qualified scholars who have worked with the available original material."[37]

The real evidence then, reveals an upright walking Hominid with a brain size one third of that found in humans but with a pelvis resembling our own. Does the Watchtower Society really believe that if such creatures were found today that "no one would call them ape-men," and that they would simply be put in zoos with other apes? From the description given by Dr. Loring Brace, it is hard to imagine a better "ape-man."

Another quote that the Watchtower Society is fond of using comes from the New York Times and once again surfaces in the creation book:

"The known fossil remains of man's ancestors would fit on top of a billiard table. That makes a poor platform from which to peer into the mists of the last few million years."[38]

I have in front of me the book *Lucy, the Beginnings of Humankind* by Donald Johanson and Maitland Edey, (quoted from six times in the creation book) which has on page 221 a photograph showing fossils removed from only one site and carrying the caption:

"The Hadar fossil collection, together at last, is

spread out in the new Cleveland laboratory to give an idea of its size and diversity."[39]

The illustration is of an extremely large table or series of tables, (a giant's billiard table perhaps) covered with fossils. The account actually relates that one of the most serious problems faced by the project was finding a location large enough to house all the fossils, and these from only one site of excavation. Did the Watchtower Society miss this photograph in their research which produced six quotations from this very book? Or was this picture, which put the lie to the New York Times reference, simply ignored because it did not fit with their intended purpose? The reader may judge.

The creation book also drags the red herring of scientific fraud across the trail. After exposing the Piltdown Man hoax, the book makes the following comments:

"In another instance, an apelike "missing link" was drawn up and presented in the press. But it was later acknowledged that the "evidence" consisted of only one tooth that belonged to an extinct form of pig."[40]

This reference is obviously to the so-called "Nebraska Man." The implication is that it was an attempt by scientists to construct an ape-man which was later discredited. But what is the true story?

The "press" in this case was the London Illustrated News of June 24 1922. The story was fabricated by the writers of the magazine and was actually discredited by the scientists who discovered the original teeth fossils. This has been established for over 70 years. Why then do the Watchtower Society use this example as if it demonstrated scientific fraud? Obviously so that a basis may be laid from which all ape-man reconstructions can be dismissed as meaningless. This is demonstrated by the conclusion stated in the very next paragraph of the creation book:

"If ape-man reconstructions are not valid..."[41]

This is typical of Watchtower Society argumentation. A couple of vague or ambiguous examples are briefly alluded to, and then a broad and sweeping conclusion is drawn. It is clear that the purpose of the Watchtower Society is determined well before any research is done. Any evidence that is uncovered not serving the purpose is ignored or misrepresented.

How different this is from the stated aim of the publication that:

"It presents a thoroughly researched examination of how life got here..."[42]

The Watchtower Society seem to have their own standards in judging what constitutes thorough research.

The only reasonable conclusion to my mind is that the Watchtower Society in publishing the creation book simply desired a vehicle to further its own propaganda without any real thought of presenting a balanced discussion of the topic. It has been my experience that the majority of people affirming a belief in evolution have never really examined the subject nor would take the time to research the assertions made in a book of this sort. The principle aim of the publication is to capitalise on this and establish confidence in the Bible's account of creation so that subsequent discussions may proceed along the lines of Watchtower theology.

Although my own views on the evolution-creation debate are not fully formed, I cannot sanction the repeated attacks made by the Watchtower Society on the competence, integrity and honesty of the scientific community. Alan Rogerson in his work Millions Now Living Will Never Die - A Study of Jehovah's Witnesses makes this observation:

"A long acquaintance with the literature of the Witnesses leads one to the conclusion that they live in the intellectual 'twilight zone'. That is, most of their members, even their leaders, are not well educated and not very intelligent. Whenever their literature strays into the fields of philosophy, academic theology, science or any severe mental discipline their ideas at best mirror popular misconceptions, at worst they are completely nonsensical."[43]

It has not been my experience that the Witnesses as a group are less intelligent than the general population that surrounds them. It does appear, however, that to a large extent they have lost their capacity for critical thinking. By allowing the Society to present both sides of every controversy and then permitting themselves to be led mentally toward the conclusions that inevitably follow, the individual Witnesses forfeit their objectivity. It is this lack of objectivity that induces them to heap praise on such a frivolous and misleading work as the creation book, and to consume ancient myth as pseudo-scientific reality.

A Question of Inerrancy

"Where it is a duty to worship the sun
it is pretty sure to be a crime to examine
the laws of heat."

John Morley

It seems to me an unfortunate business that people in general don't question more closely the things they hear or are asked to believe. Bigotry, intolerance and indifference all feed from this banquet of credulity.

It is also obvious to me that nowhere is this more true than in the arena of religion. Much injustice has been committed in the name of God and one wonders why those involved have not been able to see their actions for what they were. Appealing to the Bible as justification might have been persuasive but it cannot serve to excuse actions such as the crusades and inquisitions in which the basic rights of individuals were set as inferior to a religious and political philosophy.

I have already spoken of my discomfort with the central tenet of the Witnesses that the majority must perish for the good of the few. It appears once again that the rights of those who are designated for death are not figured into the equation. I recall a discussion with one particular Witness to whom I expressed this concern. His reply was that as these people would die anyway (eventually of old age) it would be merely a technicality if they were removed sooner. This ignores the fact that they *are* alive and have the right to live out their life without interference. It obviously reveals a very cynical view of the human race, and one not necessarily shared by all Witnesses, but what disturbed me greatly were the Biblical examples used by Witnesses to support this doctrine.

The Witnesses, in common with other fundamentalists, take the Bible to be inerrantly the word of God, free from error and infallible. If one examines the Old Testament within this constraint, a picture of a very different God to the one found in the New Testament emerges. To illustrate my point I will use just a few of the many examples available.

God's dealings with the Israelites paint him as very cruel and vicious. For example a man was able to beat his slave with a stick and if the slave lingered near death for a day or two and then finally died, no action was to be taken against the slave owner for the slave was "his property." (Exodus 21:20-21)

A child who cursed or hit his parents was to be

executed (Exodus 21:15-17). Anyone that blasphemed God must be executed (Leviticus 24:16). The penalty for harming another was "eye for eye and tooth for tooth" which meant literally that the offender's eye was to be poked out if he damaged the eye of another. (Leviticus 24:19-20)

If a "spirit of jealousy" came upon a man, he could order that his wife undergo a ritual of drinking a poisoned potion. If the woman died, she was assumed to be guilty. (Numbers 5:11-31) One wonders how many women died as a result of the unfounded suspicions of their jealous husbands. Women in any case held little authority or position and were numbered among a man's goods in the Ten Commandments. (Exodus 20:17)

God was revealed as a "warrior" (Exodus 15:3) who fought for the Israelites and who slew every firstborn in the houses of Egypt in order that everyone would see the distinction between the Israelites and the Egyptians (Exodus 11:4-7).

This "warrior" God then decreed that all non-Israelite nations must be destroyed outright. The Midianites, for example were slain entirely including women, children and the aged with only the virgins being kept "for yourselves" according to Moses' instruction (Numbers 31).

The man Samson, a judge of Israel, a hero in his battles against the Philistines and a man dedicated by his parents from birth as a Nazirite or specially consecrated one would be disfellowshiped by the Witnesses for his actions today. He many times was careless toward his Nazirite vow. He secretly disobeyed the prohibition of approaching a dead body,[1] he had immoral relations with a Gaza prostitute,[2] (whether the Watchtower Society care to admit it or not) and with Delilah.[3]

He is portrayed in the Bible account as a headstrong young man with little or no self control. Every major crisis in his life resulting in clashes with the Philistines was brought about by his relationships with Philistine women. His rash acts placed others in danger and cost them their lives.[4] He did not shy away from animal cruelty, on one occasion tying three hundred foxes together in pairs with a burning torch between their tails.[5] He disobeyed God's law and entered into a mixed marriage with a woman from among Israel's bitter enemies in defiance of his parent's wishes.[6] His life was ultimately ruined because of his insistence on having everything he wanted.

Are these the exploits of a man of God? Can we imagine such a man as a disciple of Jesus 1100 years later? Or was he a hero simply because of his prowess as a warrior in the midst of a violent society?

The Israelites, from any other perspective but their own, were a marauding band of savage looters and killers not different from the nations that surrounded them except for the fact that they regarded themselves to be God's chosen people. Their destiny then, was in God's hands and their actions justifiable as his will. I cannot accept that their actions reflected God's will for them or that God approved of their murderous course.

I shudder at the account related in Joshua chapter

seven as Israel's defeat by the men of Ai is traced to the sin of the one man Achan. As a consequence he is executed by the barbaric method of stoning, together with his daughters and his sheep and oxen, following which everything he owned is burned. How foreign is this notion of collective responsibility of the Israelites when contrasted to the New Testament concept of individual accountability. Is this the same "warrior" God as the "Prince of Peace" of the New Testament? I cannot reconcile this in my mind.

End of the world examples

My anguish with a literal interpretation of these passages was compounded by the fact that the Witnesses use examples from the Old Testament that in my mind paint God as harsh and merciless in defense of their Armageddon doctrine.

The flood of Noah's day:

When discussing his second coming, Jesus Christ in the book of Matthew made this observation to his followers:

"For the coming of the Son of Man will be just like the days of Noah. For as in those days which were before the flood they were eating and drinking, they were marrying and giving in marriage, until the day that Noah entered the ark, and they did not understand until the flood came and took them all away; so shall the coming of the Son of Man be."[7] (NAB)

The Watchtower Society refers to this passage to

confirm that God wiped out an entire world once, and he will do it again leaving only the Witnesses to survive and enjoy a new world. Certainly, those to whom Jesus spoke would have been familiar with the account of the flood. They would have understood from this illustration that Christ would come at a time that was unsuspected. They would have also understood that some individuals would refuse to acknowledge Christ's rule over them. But can we, living two thousand years later, really construe from this illustration that the vast majority of earth's inhabitants must die to grant religious freedom to a mere handful of Jehovah's Witnesses? I think not.

The Witnesses are fond of pointing out that in Jesus' illustration the populace is behaving just as today being occupied with the daily affairs of life. The fact that the majority ignore the message of the Witnesses makes the comparison even closer in their minds. But is it really just or moral to exterminate people because they don't subscribe to a specific philosophy? The answer appears to be yes, providing we perceive the philosophy to be God's.

And how does it become God's philosophy? By a particular interpretation of the Bible. Hence we have a circular argument which postulates that a particular religious group is right because they have God on their side and they know that God is on their side because their doctrines are right. This circular reasoning only appears to make sense to those holding the simplistic and narrow world view postulated by the Watchtower Society.

But to return to the question of whether it is just or moral to condemn those who disagree with our lifestyle, consider people and their pets. What would be the attitude of the majority to an individual that acquired a dog as a companion and allowed it to breed repeatedly with the local dogs and then simply killed the offspring each time? Although this undoubtedly happens, most would not approve of such action and indeed many in this position try hard to secure good homes for the litter.

In the Witnesses' scenario which involves, not animals, but human beings, we are asked to believe that God who has permitted people to multiply and build lives for themselves, is now going to terminate the vast majority en masse because they don't suit his purpose. It seems extraordinary that anyone could sanction such a destruction of individuals with feelings and free will, both of which are claimed to be God-given faculties.

The nation of Israel

As we have seen, the nation of Israel was convinced of its destiny as God's chosen people. The Witnesses point to the Israelites repeatedly in an attempt to demonstrate that God dealt with only one nation of the earth at that time.[8] The modern day Witnesses feel that their organisation is the only one directed and approved by God today.[9] The very fact that Israel took over the promised land by force three and a half thousand years ago fits well with their view that force will be required once again on their behalf as "spiritual Israelites."

But do the events related in the Bible really describe methods condoned by God? Did God really decide that the best way for Israel to take possession of the promised land was to turn the Israelites into a band of warriors and then send them on a wholesale slaughter of the land's inhabitants? Yet this is what the Watchtower Society insist happened.

There are many aspects to this that disturb me. Firstly, how could entire nations be judged as worthy of death? Surely we must allow that some good exists among nations if not within every individual. Did the God that "so loved the world that he gave his only begotten son"[10] think so little of people only fifteen hundred years prior that he condoned their destruction as whole nations? And secondly, even allowing this to be true, why turn his own people into barbarians to do the slaughtering? Could not the nations and any memory of them be simply erased by the Almighty, leaving the land empty, ready for possession by a peace loving people?

It appears far more rational to my mind that the accounts in the Bible of Israel's exploits are simply a chronicle of their efforts to conquer the people occupying land that they wished to posses. When Israel lost, they lost not because God was displeased with them but simply because in the business of war one rarely wins every battle. God was no more pleased with their smashing the heads of the Edomite children against the rocks[11] than he is with the multitude of barbaric acts that have followed down to our very day, practiced in his name.

It has been an unfortunate consequence of this literal interpretation of the Bible that justification has been given to all manner of savagery throughout history. Wars have been waged to satisfy the nationalistic ambitions of some with appeals to Bible examples and individuals have been burned alive for practices condemned by a literal interpretation of the Bible.

This literal explication presents me with a God I cannot believe in, sanctioning actions that I find repugnant.

The Garden of Eden

Another section of the Bible that causes me great difficulty is the first three chapters of Genesis. Once again the Witnesses accept (and are required to accept) these chapters as a literal historic account and refer to them as an explanation for the origin of all wickedness in the earth.

The account deals, as we have touched on previously, with the creation of all things including man and woman, the first sin and the subsequent expulsion of the pair from the garden and God's favour. Most would be familiar with the Genesis story of the "tree of the knowledge of good and evil" and its prohibition to the first couple. The command not to eat the fruit of this tree was laid upon Adam but the Devil in the guise of a serpent tricked Eve into eating the fruit which caused their fall from grace. As they were now sinners, all of their offspring were conceived in sin and thus wickedness entered the world.

If we allow this account to relate actual historical events, it presents our minds with many difficulties. The Watchtower Society makes much of the fact that the Bible asserts the first human couple to be perfect, sinless. The Society claims that Eve (who apparently received the divine prohibition regarding the fruit second hand from her husband) made a free will decision to disobey God.[12] In what appears to be a contradiction, it also points out that according to the apostle Paul, Eve was deceived by the Devil and so she ate what was forbidden to her.[13] The result of her actions is that every man woman and child carries her guilt in the form of sinfulness leading eventually to death. I cannot accept this.

Let us for the moment accept that the Genesis account is historically accurate as the Watchtower Society insists it must be. Now, Eve was either deceived or she was not. She either made an informed decision or she did not. It appears to me that these two postulates are mutually exclusive, one cannot at the same time be making an informed decision while being deceived.

If we assume that Eve was deceived into eating the forbidden fruit, does this not argue for leniency in her punishment? Especially as she apparently received the divine injunction second hand which is never as forceful or persuasive as the original. More to the point, if she was deceived, can we really point to her actions as a legitimate justification for all the thousands of years of untold suffering and misery that mankind has endured? To my mind this appears much less than perfect justice.

If, on the other hand, she was not deceived but made a free choice to disobey God, was it really an informed choice? Could she have had any idea of the suffering that future generations would experience in times of war and famine, as the victims of disease and crime? Did she really even understand the concept of death as in her experience no human had ever died? To argue that all the suffering and misery of the world has resulted from the actions of one woman and that this is somehow just in the sight of God is outrageous in my view.

The Watchtower Society further argues that the time period from Eve's sin until now has been allowed by God to prove a point, namely, that his rule is superior to man's. This surely casts the Almighty in a very poor light. Even we as mere mortals are reduced to tears when we see television footage of starving and dying children in third world countries. How long would we permit this to continue if it was within our power to stop the suffering? Can we really imagine the one described in the book of Deuteronomy as:

"A God of faithfulness and without injustice,"[14]

looking down on this wretchedness, century after century without calling a halt? Even as imperfect parents we warn our children not to play with matches. Would we think it just and fair if they ignored us and set themselves alight? Would we stand back and watch them burn in order to demonstrate that our counsel was correct? Such actions would merit criminal charges against us. How could we believe that a just and merciful God would behave in a similar manner? Only if we dispense with our critical thinking.

This literal interpretation of Genesis paints us into a moral corner from where we must engage in the most convoluted mental gymnastics to extract ourselves. It suggests a God that is vindictive, savage, and callous to the suffering of others. A God who is content to toy with the lives of men and women who are merely pawns in a game that can have only one outcome. A God that is such a poor strategist that he cannot formulate a better plan than one which involves the untimely death of billions of innocent humans. I cannot respect such a God, nor am I drawn to worship him.

Unfortunately, within the Watchtower Society community there is no room for one who does not accept a literal belief in the scriptures. When one begins to question even a portion of the Bible the Watchtower Society's whole doctrinal structure is weakened. Inevitably, this process creates more questions than it answers and so the doubter is treading on the thin ice of uncertainty rather than the solid ground of Witness dogma.

It has been an interesting phenomenon that many of the Witnesses to whom I have expressed my doubts along these lines have been comfortable to stick with the Witness world view even though they held personal doubts because it is an all-embracing philosophy. The common response is "I know it's the truth, I guess we just don't have all the answers." This of course is another circular argument and one that I was caught up in for many years until the weight of the unanswered questions overturned that which seemed established.

I have reached the stage, finally, where I am more comfortable with unanswered questions than with questionable answers.

Separate From the World

"To understand the world is wiser than to condemn it. To study the world is better than to shun it. To use the world is nobler than to abuse it. To make the world better, lovelier, and happier, is the noblest work of man or woman."

Francois Duc de la Rochefoucauld

Jehovah's Witnesses see themselves at once as both in the world and yet no part of it. They go to considerable length to demonstrate that they are only temporary residents in this world's society. To this end they don't vote in political elections nor do their school children salute the country's flag or sing the national anthem. They are careful to avoid the fashion trends of the world and do not seek association with non Witnesses. Secular and religious holidays hold no special meaning for them and they do not celebrate Christmas, birthdays, Easter, or days honouring individuals such as mother's and father's day, ANZAC day etc. Smoking and non prescription drug taking is prohibited within their ranks, as is accepting blood transfusions or products derived from blood. They refuse to perform military service of any kind even in times of peace and many will not join trade unions.

Witnesses will not buy lottery or raffle tickets and will not participate in any sort of gambling. Many of the world's customs are also considered offensive including standing for the national anthem, "toasting" at social functions, throwing confetti at weddings and more. Witnesses even have their own special terminology, preferring "impaled" over "crucified." "torture stake" over "cross," "Hebrew Scriptures" instead of "Old Testament" and so on. They also studiously avoid certain words such as "lucky" and euphemisms like "gee", "gosh" and "golly."

All of this serves to separate them from the community at large and to place a void between their society and the general population. A clear divide between us and them. This reinforces in the mind of the individual Witness that she is distinct and somehow different from her neighbours, and unites the membership as a whole.[1]

In this chapter I will attempt to describe the reasons behind this deliberate segregation and evaluate their validity.

Politics

As has been mentioned, in the estimation of the Watchtower Society, this world is under the express control of the Devil. This is held to be true concerning all aspects of society and in particular religion and politics. To support this view, scriptures such as 1 John 5:19 are cited:

"We know that we are children of God, and that the whole world is under the control of the evil one." (NIV)

Therefore to have any involvement whatsoever with politics is, in the mind of the Witness, to be enmeshed in the Devil's work.

Proceeding from this premise, the Witnesses will not seek or accept political office of any kind or vote in government elections. It is even considered inappropriate within the Witness community to express a view that favours one party over another.

The role of governments and their connection with the sovereignty of God and the life of an individual has been debated by Christians for centuries. The New Testament sheds some light on the relationship that is appropriate between Christians and the Governments of this world. The advice given by the Apostle Paul to the Christians in Rome indicated that the government of the day was serving a purpose as God's agent. Thus we read in Romans 13:1&2:

"Everyone must submit himself to the governing authorities, for there is no authority except that which

God has established. The authorities that exist have been established by God. Consequently, he who rebels against the authority is rebelling against what God has instituted, and those who do so will bring judgment on themselves." (NIV)

Although the Christian therefore is to submit to the authority of government, if in an extreme case the government of the day requires a Christian to disobey the law of God, what then? The example of the first century Christians is often cited in this context. When called before the Jewish High Court and ordered to stop preaching in the name of Jesus, they responded as recorded in the book of Acts 5:19:

"We must obey God rather than men!" (NIV)

It would appear reasonable that, between these two positions, an individual Christian's conscience would allow some latitude. For the Witnesses however, this is not a matter left up to independent decision. In the case of politics, as with so many other situations, we see the Watchtower Society going beyond what has been recorded in the scriptures and prescribing the position that all Witnesses must take. This has resulted in severe hardship for its members throughout the world.

In many countries this attitude toward governments has caused the work of the Watchtower Society to be banned and its adherents jailed. Many individual Witnesses in African countries have been brutally tortured and killed because the Watchtower Society (not the Bible) forbade them to buy a political card.[2] One is reminded of the Pharisees, roundly condemned by Jesus in the first century who:

"bind heavy burdens and grievous to be borne, and lay them on men's shoulders." (KJV)

The question must be asked, what right does any organisation have to interpret the scriptures in a way that puts at risk the life of its adherents, and then insist that this interpretation is God's will and is binding upon all?

Medicine

Another of the teachings of the Watchtower Society that jeopardises the lives of its followers is the total prohibition of blood transfusions. This doctrine is widely known throughout the general population and causes great controversy and debate among those to whom the sanctity of life is more important than religious dogma.

The Watchtower Society bases this most serious doctrine on three key scriptures in the Bible which I will discuss individually.

Genesis 9:4 "But you must not eat meat that has its lifeblood still in it." (NIV)

Here we find an interdiction laid on Noah and his family regarding meat that had not been bled. The Watchtower Society asserts that eating blood (as in the case of unbled meat) is essentially the same as having blood transfused into one's veins. There are a number of points that require clarification here.

Firstly, to have blood (or any other liquid) introduced into the body intravenously is not the same as "eating" in the sense used here in the Bible. Blood introduced through the veins does not serve as "food" for the body even though it may act as a life saver, as it does not pass through the digestive system. Secondly, the blood spoken of in this passage refers to animal blood. Nowhere is a reference made to human blood.

The context of this verse shows that the instruction concerned the food that was appropriate for Noah to eat, both vegetation and animal. Thirdly, it seems from my reading of this scripture that this prohibition on the eating of blood served to demonstrate that life was precious to God. Hence the animal's blood was a symbol of its life and not eating the blood along with the meat showed respect for that life. The Watchtower Society seems now to place greater emphasis on the symbol than on that for which it stands.

To allow a child to die rather than give permission for a blood transfusion is to miss the point of scripture and to show disregard for the value of human life. Finally, no other Christian group that uses the Bible as a guide for life sees any connection between this scripture and the modern practice of blood transfusions.

Leviticus 17:11+12 "For the life of a creature is in the blood, and I have given it to you to make atonement for yourselves on the altar; it is the blood that makes atonement for one's life. Therefore I say to the Israelites, "none of you may eat blood, nor may an alien living among you eat blood."" (NIV)

Once again, the points made previously regarding the scripture in Genesis apply; this text obviously refers to the eating of animal blood. It is interesting to note that even the orthodox Jews today, to whom the law was originally given, drain the animal blood from their kosher meats but see in this scripture no law prohibiting blood transfusions. The Watchtower Society demonstrates its inconsistency regarding this Bible book as in chapter three verse seventeen we find the words:

"...You must not eat any fat or any blood." (NIV)

To be consistent, the Watchtower Society would have to outlaw the consumption of fat also but we see no such ban.

Acts 15:28+29 "It seemed good to the Holy Spirit and to us not to burden you with anything beyond the following requirements: You are to abstain from foods sacrificed to idols, from blood, from the meat of strangled animals and from sexual immorality." (NIV)

The context of this scripture needs to be kept in mind. There was considerable controversy in the first century regarding which parts of the Jewish law were binding on the Gentile converts. This scripture from the book of Acts relates the decision reached in the Jerusalem assembly on this matter to the Christian congregation at that time. The real issue at stake was fellowship between Jewish and Gentile Christians.

For the Jewish Christians, the eating of blood was abhorrent and out of respect for their sensitive consciences the Gentile Christians were asked to abstain from blood. The Watchtower Society maintains that this decision is binding on all Christians down to this day. Even if we allow this to be true, the prohibition regarding blood relates to the previously discussed scriptures that were clearly dietary or ceremonial requirements for the Jews. There is quite simply no connection with the blood transfusions of our modern day. This kind of scriptural interpretation which allows such a radical position to be adopted regarding a life saving medical practice has been described as "absurd literalism."[3]

The inescapable conclusion is that the Watchtower Society by misinterpreting the scriptures, imperils the lives of its members. It must be remembered that this is not a matter left up to the individual conscience of each Witness. Any Witness who deliberately allows blood to be transfused into themselves or their children is deemed to have broken God's law and will be called to account by the organisation. It is quite possible that they will be disfellowshiped for this action, resulting in complete shunning by former friends and family.

Cases have even been reported of elderly people disfellowshiped on their death beds only days before dying because they accepted a blood transfusion.[4]

It is not widely known even among Jehovah's Witnesses that for many years the Watchtower Society also outlawed Vaccinations. The forerunner of the Awake! magazine, the Golden Age described vaccination as "this great evil" and stated that:

"Vaccination is a direct violation of the everlasting covenant that God made with Noah after the flood."[5]

This is a very unambiguous statement and one which caused the Witnesses at that time great difficulty as a certificate of vaccination had to be produced before a child could be enrolled in a public school in the United States. It is reported that witnesses would resort to devious means to obtain such a certificate, even having a small scar created with acid to simulate the vaccination mark.[6] Was this God's will for his people at this time? Obviously not, as in 1965 the Awake! magazine proclaimed a total reversal of this view when it stated on the subject of vaccinations:

"The issue for such persons is *not a religious one* but one of health risks."[7](italics added)

So, although in 1931 it was unequivocally a religious issue, by 1965 it had ceased to be such. This exhibits the fickle nature of the mind of man, not the unchanging word of God. Bear in mind that submission to the 1931 prohibition on vaccinations was presented to the Witnesses as God's will and as such strict obedience was demanded.

An equally serious and life threatening policy emerged in 1967. The Watchtower magazine of November 15 1967 banned organ transplants, describing them as "cannibalism," with the following words:

"Those who submit to such operations are thus living off the flesh of another human. That is cannibalistic. However, in allowing man to eat animal flesh Jehovah God did not grant permission for humans to try and perpetuate their lives by cannibalistically taking into their bodies human flesh, whether chewed or in the form of whole organs or body parts taken from others."[8]

This statement was later amplified to include all transplants between humans.[9] Once again we have a very clear statement, set out as God's own will for man, and couched in the strongest possible terms. Whether one agrees with the medical procedure of organ transplants is not the issue. The issue centres on whether an organisation claiming to be God's channel of communication has the right to lay an injunction on its members that imperils their very lives.

The actions of the Watchtower Society are even more disgraceful when viewed in the light of their total about-face regarding this issue. The Watchtower issue of March 15 1980 stated:

"...there is no Biblical command pointedly forbidding the taking in of other human tissue... It is a matter for personal decision.(Gal. 6:5) The congregation judicial committee would not take disciplinary action if someone accepted an organ transplant."[10]

What of the Witnesses who may have died as a result of refusing a kidney transplant or who gave up sight rather than receive a transplanted cornea? No apology is offered by the Watchtower Society for their erroneous instruction. Once again the question remains, how could an organisation that removed these decisions from the hands of its followers and then so totally reversed its position at a later date, be directed by God of whom the Apostle Paul contends:

"For God is not a God of disorder but of peace"(1 Cor. 14:33 NIV).

Clearly, the God of the Bible is much maligned by rash actions such as these, conducted in his name.

After considering these examples, one cannot help but wonder whether the current stand on blood transfusions introduced in the mid 1940s will also be reversed at some time in the future by the Watchtower Society.

*** Author's note. Again with the benefit of hindsight we are starting to see the beginnings of change. The Watchtower magazine of June 15th 2000, page 31 indicated that some blood plasma fractions which were previously prohibited may now be acceptable to Jehovah's Witnesses, determined by their own conscience-based decision. I suspect further easing of this doctrine will take place in the future.*

Celebrations

As stated earlier, Jehovah's Witnesses do not take part in what most Christians would regard as "normal" celebrations. To illustrate the kind of strange logic applied by the Watchtower Society to such issues, we will consider the example of birthdays.

The Witnesses are forbidden to celebrate birthdays including the birthdays of their children. They may not even send a birthday card or wish someone a birthday greeting. Neither will they attend a birthday party.[11] This ban is based primarily on two scriptures from the Bible which we will analyse.

Genesis 40:20-22 "Now the third day was Pharaoh's birthday, and he gave a feast for all his officials. He lifted up the heads of the chief cupbearer and the chief baker in the presence of all his officials: He restored the chief cupbearer to his position, so that he once again put the cup into Pharaohs hand, but he hanged the chief baker, just as Joseph had said to them in his interpretation." (NIV)

It is clear from this passage that the chief baker was killed at Pharaohs birthday party. The reasoning of the Watchtower Society is that since the Bible paints the birthday party as being evil in this scripture, then birthday parties should be avoided by Christians. Remember too, that this is not left to the individual Witness conscience, it is enforced as a punishable offence.

If we examine this text however, what is the source of the evil? Obviously it is the Pharaoh that is evil not the party at which the evil deed took place. In fact the Witness logic could be used equally well to support birthday parties as the Pharaoh restored the chief cupbearer to his former position at the same party, therefore birthday parties could be beneficial. Of course such reasoning is ludicrous. The argument of "guilt by association" is absurd.

Matthew 14:6-10 "On Herod's birthday the daughter of Herodias danced for them and pleased Herod so much that he promised with an oath to give her whatever she asked. Prompted by her mother she asked "Give me here on a platter the head of John the Baptist." The king was distressed, but because of his oaths and his dinner guests, he ordered that her request be granted and had John beheaded in the prison." (NIV)

The Watchtower Society teaching follows similar lines to the previous example: As Herod was a pagan and celebrated birthdays such occasions must be unsuitable for Christians. Also, as in the case of Pharaoh, a wicked deed took place at this celebration.

Once again, the "guilt by association" argument is invalid. What this text tells us is that the actions of Herod were contemptible. It tells us nothing regarding the appropriateness of the celebration for Christians.

The Watchtower Society dismiss another account in the Bible which seems to indicate that Job, a righteous man celebrated birthdays.

Job 1:4 "And his [Job's] sons went and feasted in their houses, every one his day; and sent and called for their three sisters to eat and drink with them" (KJV) Reading the context we see that Job himself is present at these feasts.

The Living Bible renders this verse this way:

"Every year when Job's sons had birthdays, they invited their brothers and sisters to their homes for a celebration. On these occasions they would eat and drink with great merriment."

The Bible Knowledge Commentary volume one by Walvoord and Zuck tells us:

"Each time his seven sons held a feast (possibly a birthday party) in one of their homes along with their ... sisters"[12]

To be fair, these feasts held on each one's "day" are not explicitly named as birthday parties in many versions of the Bible. The quotations given however (and many more could be provided) demonstrate that there is a strong possibility that the God-fearing man Job did indeed celebrate birthdays. This being the case, it must surely be up to an individual Christian's conscience as to whether she celebrates this occasion.

Nevertheless the Watchtower Society, true to

form, takes a hard line and legislates that its adherents do not participate in this innocent pleasure. I have yet to see a child emotionally scarred by attending a birthday party. I have however, seen many people badly damaged by attempting to hold to the Watchtower Society's inane teachings, believing they are doing God's will.

The Cross

As mentioned at the beginning of this chapter, the Watchtower Society insist that Jesus did not die on a cross as is usually depicted but instead died on an upright wooden pole. Further to this they claim that the cross is in fact a pagan symbol, the use of which identifies a religion to be from the Devil. This serves the useful purpose of separating them from most other religions that use the symbol of the cross in their worship.

The Watchtower Society point out that the Greek word stauros was often used to refer to the Roman instrument of execution which most commonly is called the cross. The primary meaning of this Greek word refers to an upright pole or stake,[13] so the Society maintains that Jesus died on such an upright pole without a crossbeam. In accord with this interpretation, the New World Translation of the Holy Scriptures uses "impaled" instead of "crucified" and "torture stake" instead of "cross" throughout.

As is their habit, however, the Watchtower Society

have not told the whole story. Robert Bowman, a specialist in cultic writings makes this observation regarding the Greek word stauros:

"In truth, the cross could and did take on a variety of shapes, notably those similar to the Greek letter tau (T) and the plus sign (+), occasionally using two diagonal beams (X), as well as (infrequently) a simple upright stake with no crosspiece. To argue that only the last-named form was used, or that stauros could be used only for that form, is contradictory to the actual historical facts and is based on a naive restriction of the term to its original or simplest meaning."[14]

Supporting this clarification, the Hollman Bible Dictionary informs us that:

"Four types of crosses were used: 1) The Latin cross has the crossbeam about two thirds of the way up the upright pole; 2) St. Anthony's cross (probably due to its similarity with his famous crutch) had the beam at the top of the upright pole like a T. 3) St. Andrew's cross (supposedly used to crucify Andrew) had the shape of the letter X. 4) the Greek cross had both beams equal in the shape of a plus sign."[15]

Given the varied use of the word stauros to describe different shapes, does the Bible shed any more light on its application in the case of Jesus' death? Consider the testimony of the following two Bible texts:

John 20:25 "The other disciples therefore said unto him, [Thomas] We have seen the Lord. But he said unto them, Except I shall see in his hands the print of the nails, and put my finger into the print of the nails, and thrust my hand into his side, I will not believe." (KJV)

Note here in this scripture how many nails were used on Jesus' hands. The account quite clearly states "nails" not "nail." If the Watchtower's assertion that Jesus died on a single pole was correct, there would have been one nail used to pin Jesus' hands above his head (as illustrated in numerous Watchtower Society publications). The Bible however, refers to "the print of the nails" indicating more than one nail was used, as would be expected of someone attached to a cross with arms outstretched.

Matthew 27:37 "Above his head they placed the written charge against him: THIS IS JESUS, THE KING OF THE JEWS." (NIV)

If Jesus had died on a pole with his hands nailed over his head as the Watchtower Society asserts, the scripture should have read that the sign was placed "above his hands." (The reader is called upon to use her powers of visualisation). Instead the Bible refers to the position of this sign as being "above his head" as would be expected in the case of someone with outstretched arms. So while obviously not definitive, both of these Bible passages are consistent with the use of a traditional cross.

Now it may be argued that the actual shape of the stauros is not the important matter, but this case highlights the poor scholarship of the Watchtower Society and its pedantic stance on issues which serve only one purpose; to separate it from the mainstream churches and allow it to claim possession of unique truths.

Friendships

As has been alluded to previously, the Witnesses keep very much to themselves where associations are concerned. The Watchtower Society through its many publications teaches that it is unwise to have close attachments to non Jehovah's Witnesses and urges its adherents to seek companionship within the organisation.

The scripture found at 1 Corinthians 15:33 can be recited verbatim by almost all Jehovah's Witnesses:

"Do not be misled. Bad associations spoil useful habits." (NWT)

The Apostle Paul here likely quoted the pagan writer Menander indicating that "bad company corrupts good character." This was in the context of his discussion of the resurrection hope with the Corinthian Christians. There were those in the first century such as the Sadducees who were very materialistic in their outlook. They denied the existence of life after death or the concept of punishment or reward in another world.

Aristocratic in attitude, they opposed Jesus and claimed great knowledge although as Paul pointed out they were ignorant of God.[16] Paul then, was warning the Christians in Roman Corinth that they should avoid these false teachers and their philosophy. In discussing this particular group he was not making a general statement dividing people into good and bad categories as if everyone can be classified as either "all good" or "all bad."

Indeed, most people would see the issue of "good and bad" to be a function of individual human nature not some artificially imposed classification as the Watchtower Society would have us believe. Christians in fact are warned in the scriptures not to be making such judgments regarding a person's worth as it is not their prerogative, but God's.[17]

The Watchtower Society, however, takes a simplistic view and applies this scripture to all who are not Jehovah's Witnesses, a fact those acquainted with its publications will know. The individual Witnesses take this very seriously and they are reminded constantly of the dangers inherent in "bad associations." Witness children are encouraged not to play with non Witness children after school, even if they have no other companions of their own age.

This demonstrates to my mind the absolute authority that Witnesses confer upon their organisation. To allow the Watchtower society to define who is good and who is bad in such broad terms using flimsy scriptural argument and then to enforce that definition strictly, is to my mind socially unhealthy and mentally damaging as we will see in subsequent chapters.

Smoking

Jehovah's Witnesses may not smoke. A smoker who becomes a Witness must quit before being baptised and a Witness who takes up smoking will be disfellowshiped.

In support of this ordinance the Watchtower

Society cite scriptures such as the following:

2 Corinthians 7:1 "Since we have these promises, dear friends, let us purify ourselves from everything that contaminates body and spirit, perfecting holiness out of reverence for God." (NIV)

While it is true that smoking defiles the body and a Christian may see this scripture and others as an encouragement to stop smoking, it is the Watchtower Society, not the Bible, that turns this counsel into legislation with attendant punishment. The Witnesses are not alone in this however as Seventh Day Adventists and Mormons take a similar position and in fact extend the ban to cover alcohol, tea and coffee.[18]

In appending these requirements to the guidelines set out for Christians in the Bible, these groups undermine the scriptures as being incomplete or inadequate for daily life. The Apostle Paul himself showed that the keeping of certain dietary regulations as did the Jews was no longer a requisite for Christian living:

"Therefore do not let anyone judge you by what you eat or drink, or with regard to a religious festival, a New Moon celebration or a Sabbath day." Colossians 2:16 (NIV)

The issue of course is not whether there are health benefits in abstaining from certain foods or practices. What is at dispute is whether an organisation of men has the right to impose an additional layer of requirements upon its followers and then insist that this is God's will for them.

All of the things discussed in this chapter, and many more not mentioned, create an artificial separation between the community of Jehovah's Witnesses and the rest of society. The circular reasoning involved is evident from the fact that once this separation from the mainstream churches as well as society in general is achieved by means of the Watchtower Society's unique doctrines, the very fact of this separation is then cited as evidence of God's blessing and choosing. While the Witnesses may point to some benefits that this segregation brings, it is my view that the disadvantages in terms of mental health and stability outweigh these as I will discuss in the next two chapters.

When Things Go Wrong

"Whatever the party holds to be truth
is truth. It is impossible to see
reality except by looking through the
eyes of the party."

George Orwell

With this chapter, I will begin looking closely at some of the more pernicious aspects of the Watchtower Society as I see them. I will consider the disciplinary methods employed by the Society and the procedures followed when problems arise. As I draw heavily on my own experiences, I must of necessity relate them also.

At the outset, it is important to recognise that the Watchtower Society requires the unquestioning obedience of all Witnesses. It is held up to the faithful as the one channel used by God to dispense spiritual truth and so to question it is to question God. The following extracts show the kind of language used throughout this century by Watchtower Society publications to describe the organisation:

Watchtower September 15 1910:

"Furthermore, not only do we find that people cannot see the divine plan in studying the Bible by itself, but we see, also, that if anyone lays the SCRIPTURE STUDIES aside... and ignores them and goes to the Bible alone...our experience shows that within two years he goes into darkness."[1]

Watchtower February 1 1952:

"If we do not see a point at first we should keep trying to grasp it, rather than opposing it and rejecting it and presumptuously taking the position that we are more likely to be right than the discreet slave. We should meekly go along with the Lord's theocratic organisation and wait for further clarification."[2]

Qualified to be Ministers 1967:

"If we have love for Jehovah and for the organisation of his people we shall not be suspicious, but shall, as the Bible says, "believe all things," all things that The Watchtower brings out."[3]

Watchtower February 15 1981:

"If we have once established what instrument God is using as his "slave" to dispense spiritual food to his people, surely Jehovah is not pleased if we receive that food as if it might contain something harmful. We should have confidence in the channel God is using."[4]

Watchtower January 15 1983:

"Avoid independent thinking... questioning the counsel that is provided by God's visible organisation."[5]

These few examples are sufficient to establish that the organisation's instructions are synonymous with God's direction. Individual Witnesses must not think for themselves and must not question what is delivered to them through the Watchtower magazine.

But what if an individual, in all conscience, cannot accept a particular teaching of the Watchtower Society? The only course open to such a person is to keep this view to herself and if called upon publicly to defend the Society's teaching then she must do so or risk being labeled as an apostate.

In the early 1980's the Watchtower Society went through somewhat of an upheaval as it attempted to quash major dissent taking place in senior positions. The extent to which the Society requires total conformity is illustrated in an official letter dated September 1 1980 and published in the book *Crisis of Conscience*, that was sent to all travelling representatives from the International Headquarters. The letter, on page two, contained this incredible directive:

"Keep in mind that to be disfellowshiped, an apostate does not have to be a promoter of apostate views... Extended, kindly efforts should be put forth to readjust his thinking. However, if, after such extended efforts have been put forth to readjust his thinking, he continues to believe the apostate ideas and rejects what he has been provided through the 'slave class', then appropriate judicial action should be taken."[6]

So not only one's actions but a person's own thoughts have to be subject to the Watchtower Society. This really leaves the one experiencing difficulties with little latitude for free thought. Understandably, the individual troubled by a particular doctrine of the Society needs to be very careful to whom she speaks.

This was exactly the position in which I increasingly found myself during my last few years with the Witnesses. I was having great difficulty reconciling many Watchtower doctrines with the Bible and with science. I was particularly distressed by the concept of the deaths of all who were not Witnesses at Armageddon (the final war between God and man, the subject of many failed prophecies by the Watchtower Society as we've seen). In my daily life I came across many good people, both Christian and non-Christian.

These people seemed to my mind no different from the Witnesses I knew in that they were concerned for the welfare of their children, upset by the injustice of the world and had a caring attitude toward their fellow man etc. The only real difference that I could discern was that they did not follow the Watchtower Society's interpretation of the Bible. I could not understand why they deserved to die, or even why God would want to kill them.

I was troubled too by the level of interference that the Society imposed on people's lives. Many decisions that should have been made by the individual were being taken by the Society without any real scriptural backing and as an Elder I felt duty bound to support the party line although I felt it to be wrong. I saw people becoming ill due to the guilt of not achieving the targets of hours dictated by the Society for time spent in the door to door service. I felt stupid and childish trying to defend the Society's position on such things as birthdays, blood transfusions and their preposterous chronology.

The five weekly meetings too, were taking their toll as there we were reminded again and again of the miserable plight of the world and of those outside the organisation. The same tedious doctrines are served up in different disguises year in year out until the individual loses totally her perspective of reality.

At these meetings information is considered slowly and ponderously so that none will miss the points that the Society wish absorbed. This creates the illusion that what is being considered is complex and weighty and requires great thought and attention, while in most cases it is absurdly simplistic and shallow. There were times when I wanted to scream out that "We've heard all this stuff a million times with different garnishes and we're choking to death on it!"

It became more and more of a strain as time progressed and my fear of other's reactions left me few people in whom I felt I could confide. The problem was exacerbated by the fact that public "witnessing" or preaching from door to door is required of all Witnesses on a regular basis, and I as an Elder had to set the lead. I found myself hating the weekends because I knew I would have to go from door to door attempting to convince people of things in which even I had no confidence.

More often than not I would wake on the weekend with a crippling headache. To leave the organisation, however, is to abandon the entire family and social network that has been built up in a Witness's life over many years and this cannot be undertaken hastily.

The stress of this dissonance led to physical sickness and enormous mental anguish. A great strain was placed on my family and particularly on my relationship with my wife who was wholly committed to the Witness lifestyle and feared that if I slowed down in my service to the organisation I would leave it. Her constant encouragement for me to continue, despite the damage that I knew it to be causing me, I interpreted as yet more pressure to conform to a lifestyle that I was coming to despise. My inability to isolate my relationship with her from the organisation she served eventually led to our separation.

The pressure of living with this dissonance came to a head in November of 1992. Physically weakened by a viral infection, I just seemed to collapse inside and I knew I could not face another day as a Jehovah's Witness. Unable to stop crying, I was taken to our family doctor who immediately confined me to hospital for a week. It was while in hospital that I decided things must change. Albeit by nature a reasonably calm person, I had been troubled for months by thoughts of suicide. Every day, and sometimes many times each day I would think of how easy it would be just to go to sleep and not wake up again to face my problems.

As hard as I tried, I could not stop these thoughts and was becoming very afraid. Although I knew inside that my problems stemmed from the difficulties I was having with Watchtower Society doctrine, many of my Witness friends were telling me that I was suffering from a chemical imbalance in the brain and needed medical help. I began to doubt my own sanity. To his credit, my doctor insisted that I make plans to do something about my problems while assuring me that I was not going insane or in need of drug therapy.

Still without the courage to totally separate myself from the Witnesses, I resigned my position as an Elder, against the advice of many others. This provided temporary relief, but still the obligation to teach others what I no longer believed, remained. Finally, in July of 1993 I decided that I would cease to be an active Witness. In June 1994 by means of a letter, I formally disassociated myself from the organisation.

One could be forgiven, after reading my account, for asking why I did not leave sooner. To understand why, one needs to appreciate the might of the big stick with which the Society keeps its members in line.

Disfellowshiping

Sir Sarvepalli Radhakrishnan, an Indian philosopher and statesman, once said of organised religion:

"It is not God that is worshipped but the group or authority that claims to speak in his name. Sin becomes disobedience to authority not violation of integrity."[7]

Within the Witness community, this sin of disobedience is punished by disfellowshiping.

To be disfellowshiped is to be excommunicated or put out of the Witnesses' organisation. Tens of thousands of Witnesses are disfellowshiped each year.[8] In my opinion, after seeing the effects of many disfellowshipings, this mechanism is the most unkind and un-Christian teaching of the Watchtower Society.

To justify such action, the Watchtower Society appeals to the Bible.

2 John 10-11 "If anyone comes to you and does not bring this teaching, do not take him into your house or welcome him. Anyone who welcomes him shares in his wicked work" (NIV)

Matthew 18:17 "...and if he refuses to listen even to the church, treat him as you would a pagan or a tax collector" (NIV)

1 Corinthians 5:11 "But now I am writing to you that you must not associate with anyone who calls himself a brother but who is sexually immoral or greedy, an idolater or a slanderer, a drunkard or a swindler. With such a man do not even eat." (NIV)

It cannot be denied that the scriptures warn against individuals that promote heresy and destructive teachings. The congregation also needs to be protected against those who by their deliberate actions seek to corrupt it.

The Watchtower Society however, uses these basic first century teachings to control any who diverge from its own interpretation of the Bible. Thus someone who considers herself a Christian and has a love for God, but for example, who accepts a blood transfusion, will be put out of the organisation. This surely was not the intent of scripture.

It does serve however, as a powerful deterrent in the minds of those troubled by Watchtower dicta. The effect of this action on a disfellowshiped person's life must not be underestimated. If the disfellowshiped person has been a Witness for some time, it is unlikely that she will have any friends outside the organisation for reasons that we have already discussed. When the disfellowshiping action takes place and is announced publicly, none of her former Witness friends will associate with her any longer. They themselves are threatened with disfellowshiping if they do so.

If the disfellowshiped one has been raised a Witness (as many are) and thus has Witness relatives, then this injunction extends to those Witness family members also. If the family members are not living under the same roof they are encouraged to have only contact that is unavoidable with their disgraced relative.

Wives with disfellowshiped husbands are forbidden to discuss anything of a spiritual nature with their spouse and vice versa.[9] The disfellowshiped one is not welcome in the homes of Witnesses and will not even be acknowledged on the street if she passes one of her former "brothers" or "sisters."

Thus the disfellowshiped one finds herself all alone in the world. Chances are that her mind has been poisoned by her time with the organisation to the extent that she views all non Witnesses with deep suspicion even though she is now in the same category. Because of this fact, she may find it very difficult to make new friends and the constant shunning by her old friends reinforces her feelings of guilt.

It is not surprising then that many seek to return to the organisation, acknowledging their "wrong" course and may eventually be "reinstated" following a long period of humiliation. Unless one has been through this transition from accepted and valued member of a close knit community to persona non grata, one cannot understand the mental suffering that takes place. In my own case, I left the organisation willfully and fully cognisant of the difficulties that I would face and still it was distressing for me. Others who are forcibly removed experience even more mental anguish in adjusting to their new life.

The disfellowshiping process has a sobering affect on those who remain inside the organisation also. As they can no longer communicate with their fallen "brother" or "sister" they have to trust that the organisation did the right and fair thing. A very dim view is taken of any Witness that dares to question the actions of the Watchtower Society in these matters. The society's publications are used to make this point:

Watchtower January 1 1983:

"If someone is disfellowshiped, he must at the time have had a truly bad heart and/or been determined to pursue a God-dishonouring course. Peter said that the condition of such a person is worse than before he became a Christian; he is like 'a sow that was bathed but has gone back to the mire' (2 Peter 2:20-22) This should help Christian relatives and others to have God's view of a disfellowshiped person."[10]

The subtext is that even if the disfellowshiped person's former friends are troubled by her expulsion, they should trust the organisation and believe that their former "sister" has "a truly bad heart." The Watchtower's position on this is once again presented as God's own. I personally find such language offensive.

It is interesting to note that in former years, when an announcement was made to the congregation regarding a disfellowshiping action, the reason for the action was given as "conduct unbecoming a Christian" on the part of the expelled one. This has since been changed as some who were disfellowshiped brought legal action against the Watchtower Society and argued successfully that the Society's definition of "un-Christian conduct" was invalid. Now an announcement is simply made that the person has been disfellowshiped but with no reference to their conduct.

Also of interest is the way the situation is presented to the Witnesses who remain within the organisation. The disfellowshiped person and not the congregation must carry the blame for the anguish now created by the expulsion:

Watchtower September 15 1981:

"...the conduct of the wrongdoer has changed his relationship with Jehovah and therefore with his family who are Jehovah's Witnesses."[11]

Watchtower January 1 1983:

"We may not be able to undo all the hurt or make up for all the loss that the disfellowshiped person has caused his Christian relatives.."[2]

Hence the Witness community does not have to feel remorse for cutting off their former friend as they are persuaded to place the blame squarely on the shoulders of the disfellowshiped one. In reality the decision not to speak to their former friend must be theirs and theirs alone but the Watchtower Society seeks to blur this responsibility by letting the disfellowshiped person carry this decision for everyone.

Someone who formally disassociates himself from the Watchtower Society (as I did) automatically gains the status of a disfellowshiped person. This is interesting. What it really means is that an individual may choose to become a Jehovah's Witness but this same individual may not choose to leave without acquiring a status that ensures none of his Witness associates will have anything further to do with him.

Whereas an individual could simply lapse and stop attending Watchtower Society meetings etc., someone making the decision that I did, namely that I no longer wanted to be recognised as a Jehovah's Witness, is automatically dumped into the same category as those expelled from the organisation for wrongdoing. This cleverly ensures that such a person no longer has the capacity to discuss their doubt with other Witnesses. I'm quite confident that if the Watchtower Society thought it could stop the distribution of books such as this, it would do that also. Within the walls of the Watchtower Society community, God's Justice is elevated above his mercy.

The process of disfellowshiping also demonstrates the conditional nature of friendships within the Witness community. It is ironic that the Watchtower Society actually highlights the kind of shallow friendships that it claims occur in the "world" in contrast with those to be found within the organisation as the following Watchtower extract demonstrates:

"Many people, nevertheless, claim that they do have friends. But how much depth is there to such relationships? Often a person takes an interest in someone because of what that one has to offer, not because of what he is."[13]

This is exactly the case within the Witness community. As long as an individual is in favour with the organisation, then her "brothers and sisters" will pledge their undying allegiance. But if the former friend should be unfortunate enough to be disfellowshiped or should choose to leave the organisation, all ties are severed. It no longer matters that the person may have redeeming qualities, she no longer has anything to offer the organisation. When it is all boiled down, what an individual is, what values the individual holds, comes a poor second to their continuing obedience to the Watchtower Society.

It matters not whether a person has served for twenty or thirty years and has put family or career on hold during this time. If one differs from the official Watchtower Society position, friends suddenly become thin on the ground.

It appears that in the matter of true friendships, the Watchtower Society has less to boast of than it might imagine. What though, is to be done with someone who, while not committing actions that merit disfellowshiping, is seen to behave in ways that run counter to the Watchtower Society's guidelines?

Marking

"Marking" is the process by which individual Witnesses can begin to cut off associations with the offending member while she is still part of the congregation. This process was established by the Apostle Paul in his second letter to the Christians in Thessalonica:

"If anyone does not obey our instruction in this letter, take special note of him. Do not associate with him, in order that he may feel ashamed." (2 Thess. 3:14 NIV)

The context of this scripture shows that Paul, while commending the Christians in Thessalonica for their faithfulness to Christ despite persecution, had heard reports of confusion among the faithful due to false teaching on the subject of the day of the Lord. Paul's counsel was to bring social pressure upon the ones holding to this false teaching so that they may become ashamed and repent.

The Watchtower Society now claim that not only does this scripture have a general application to one disobedient to the Bible's counsel, but also to anyone disobedient to its own counsel as God's mouthpiece.

In this context, the Society's book *Organised to Accomplish our Ministry* instructed:

"Even though no name has been mentioned, individual members of the congregation would then be obliged to "mark" a person, or persons, of that kind, just as Paul advised the brothers in Thessalonica. If the disorderly one should still persist in his wayward course of conduct, he remains in grave danger of eventually committing a serious sin that could lead to his being disfellowshiped."[14]

So there are mechanisms in place to control not only those who break God's law but also anyone that disputes the Watchtower Society's interpretation of that law.

The Witnesses are constantly reminded that God is able to "read the hearts" and "discern the thoughts" of any individual and because of this, any wickedness, though hidden will be revealed. They are told that if wrongdoing on the part of another Witness comes to their attention, they must report it to the Elders. Failing to do so results in the observer having a share in the sin.[15] This provides an extensive spy network within the Society with every person duty bound to report perceived wrongdoing.

All of this, combined with the Society's continual elaboration on the wretched condition of those in the world serves to mark clearly the boundary of the Witness community. One is either inside, or outside. Those within are friends, can be trusted, are specially favoured by God and can be relied upon to fight shoulder to shoulder for the faith.

On the other hand, those outside are in spiritual

darkness, are untrustworthy, have minds twisted by "worldly" thinking and are a constant threat to a Christian's spirituality. The apparatus that regularly reinforces this view is both elaborate and pervasive. It is little wonder that many Witnesses simply cannot step back and see the "big picture" with the Watchtower Society as one tiny element.

A Dangerous Perspective

"It is with nations as with individuals,
those who know the least of others
think the highest of themselves; for
the whole family of pride and ignorance
are incestuous and mutually beget
each other."

Caleb C. Colton

I have stated repeatedly that in my opinion, the Watchtower Society's policies, interpretations and directions are damaging to the mental health and general stability of its members.

In this chapter I will describe some of the damage I have seen done to Witness's thinking and demonstrate that they are left ill equipped to function properly as members of society in general. I will also attempt to explain why the perspective adopted by the Watchtower Society is dangerous, both to the individual Witness and to the wider community.

Steve Hassan, a former member of the Unification Church commonly known as the "Moonies," authored a book in which he described the mind control methods used on the movements' adherents. He recounts:

"The essence of mind control is that it encourages dependence and conformity, and discourages autonomy and individuality... [it seeks] to undermine an individual's integrity in making his own decisions... the ideology is internalised as "the truth," the only "map" of reality. All that is good is embodied in the group... All that is bad is on the outside... there is never a legitimate reason for leaving... Members are told that the only reasons why people leave are weakness, temptation, insanity, brainwashing,... pride, sin and so on."[1]

These methods, common in organisations employing mind control are all to be found within the Watchtower Society, and indeed, we have already discussed several of these methods as employed by the Society. The affects on one's thinking resulting from these tactics do not automatically stop when one leaves the movement. Australian psychologist Louise Samways comments in her book *Dangerous Persuaders*:

"Without professional help mind control can be extremely difficult to undo, even when the person has left the group and wants to change."[2]

Let us consider some additional ways in which the mind of the individual Witness is affected by her association with the Watchtower Society.

The artificial world

I have spoken already about the isolated manner in which the Witnesses live as part of the community. The Watchtower Society's literature is used repeatedly to remind them of this separation. They are encouraged to shelter within "the safety of God's organisation," appreciate the blessings of "the spiritual paradise," steer clear of the "dangers of this old system of things" and "work shoulder to shoulder" with God's organisation as the "nucleus of the New World society."

The individual Witnesses are then assailed with a flood of literature which gives advice and direction on every aspect of their lives. They are strongly encouraged to read all of this "spiritual food" before looking at anything else. Not to do so is to manifest an unappreciative attitude in the eyes of the Watchtower Society toward God's provisions.

Faced with this pressure, many Witnesses simply do not have time to read any other literature. The individual members are further insulated by the Society's counsel regarding material of a critical nature. Any literature written by an ex-member of the organisation, such as this book, is strictly taboo as an apostate work of the Devil.[3] Simply to possess it could invite the Devil into one's home and so the Watchtower Society would insist on it being burned (another parallel with the Nazis of the 1930s.) Even books dealing with higher criticism of the Bible are frowned upon due to the effect that these may have on the faith of the Witness. All of this essentially insulates the individual members of the organisation from the literature of the world and any alternative perspectives.

To ensure that the Witnesses are not distracted by extra curricular activities, a hectic program of Bible study and meeting attendance is imposed upon them by the Society. A typical schedule for the week's activity would be:

Monday:

AM Consider the daily text from the book Examining the Scriptures Daily (A small booklet with one scriptural text together with the Society's interpretation for each day of the year.)

PM Prepare material for the Theocratic Ministry School and the Service Meeting.

(It is considered to be very poor form to arrive at a meeting without at least pre-reading and underlining the key thoughts in each paragraph of the material to be considered.)

Tuesday:

AM Consider the daily text from the book Examining the Scriptures Daily.

PM Attend Theocratic Ministry School and Service Meeting (Two meetings designed to equip the Witness to undertake the preaching work from house to house. The meeting features talks, demonstrations, question and answer parts, interviews, testimonials, and discussions between two or more persons.)

Wednesday:

AM Consider the daily text from the book Examining the Scriptures Daily.

PM Prepare material for Congregation Book Study.

Thursday:

AM Consider the daily text from the book Examining the Scriptures Daily.

PM Attend and participate in the Congregation Book Study(A small meeting held in a private home using a recent Watchtower Society publication as a study text. Not a public meeting.)

Friday:

AM Consider the daily text from the book Examining the Scriptures Daily.

PM Family Bible study as required of all Witness fathers (A man will not be selected for further responsibility within the organisation if he is not regularly conducting a family Bible study.)

Saturday:

AM Consider the daily text from the book Examining the Scriptures Daily.

AM Spend two to three hours in door to door preaching activity (This activity is essential for all Witnesses. An individual will not be counted as a Witness unless she shares in this work regularly. All Witnesses are expected to participate in the preaching work weekly.)

PM Prepare for study of the Watchtower magazine

on Sunday.

Sunday:

AM Consider the daily text from the book Examining the Scriptures Daily.

AM Attend Public lecture, attend and participate in Watchtower study. (The public lecture is aimed at new Witnesses and is often the first meeting that a prospective Witness attends. At the Watchtower study an article from the Watchtower magazine is considered in a question and answer format with everyone expected to participate. The Watchtower is the principle channel used by the organisation to publish its doctrine.)

This schedule would be promoted by the Watchtower Society as a minimum requirement for maintaining spiritual health. In summer, evening door to door preaching would be added one night of the week and time must be found for personal Bible study too. To miss meetings or to attend without preparation is seen to manifest a poor attitude toward God's provisions.

With this level of activity, the individual simply does not have time to become involved with anything else. W.C. Stevenson, himself a former Witness commented in his book *Year of doom, 1975*:

"But I believe that this extraordinarily crowded schedule is the key to understanding why once someone is so far into the movement it is very difficult for him to see things in any other way than that taught by the movement."[4]

The individual Witness is also encouraged to look

within the organisation for support when experiencing difficulties. The use of outside psychologists is frowned upon and the Elders of the congregation, using Watchtower publications will attempt to help the flock with whatever problems arise.

We also find the Witness children insulated from the education system as much as possible. The general attitude seems to be that as the schools teach only knowledge of the "old world" and the associations while at school are bad, it is reasonable for the child to leave as soon as it is feasible. The goal of full time preaching is held out to children as a noble vocation straight from school. Thousands of children have done this, only to realise years later when contemplating marriage and a family that their "vocation" has left them with little or no skill to offer a prospective employer.

It is also fairly predictable that tertiary education is frowned upon. To gain higher education is seen as an attempt to secure ones future in this old world which for the Witnesses is to be short lived. The Watchtower magazine is used to highlight the dangers in the university atmosphere with comments such as:

"Some of the worst associations possible for a Christian - spiritually and morally speaking - have been found on university campuses."[5]

When all of this is combined, the individual Witness is isolated to a large extent from non Watchtower Society approved stimulus. An all encompassing paradigm is developed which serves to filter everything that the Witness encounters. This framework is the basis on which the rest of the Witnesses' life is evaluated. After a while, the individual's own inclination becomes secondary to their loyalty to the organisation and then the circle is complete.

The subjugation of will

I am aware, of course, that we are all influenced to varying degrees by the world in which we find ourselves. This is unavoidable and indeed is the aim of commercial elements who would have us buy their products as well as others who seek our sympathy for their cause.

It seems to me however, that any individual who surrenders her will to one organisation is in a precarious position. Jehovah's Witnesses, while recognising that they live no longer for themselves and have given up independent thinking, consider the Watchtower Society to be God's only channel of guidance today and are therefore largely comfortable with this situation. But what if they are wrong?

One of the problems the Witnesses face is that everything they encounter has to be fitted into the Society's framework of understanding. If something does not fit, it must simply be wrong. Many strategies have been developed to deflect any such inconsistencies. The Devil is seen by the Witnesses to be very cunning and as such has devised elaborate schemes to lure the majority of mankind over to his camp.[6]

I can remember one personal conversation with a Witness to whom I put the question "How would you feel if paleontologists uncovered a perfect set of transitional fossils linking modern man with a more primitive form?" Her response was that it would not be of concern as "It would have to be wrong." The subtext is of course that anything not fitting within the Watchtower Society's framework of understanding is simply incorrect, no matter how convincing the evidence. Once this stage is reached, (fairly rapidly in my experience) the individual is no longer objective and has been essentially brainwashed.

The language used by the New World Translation is in keeping with this process of mind control. Note the difference between the King James version of the Bible and the Society's New World Translation when discussing the issue of child discipline:

Ephesians 6:4 "And, ye fathers, provoke not your children to wrath; but bring them up in the nurture and admonition of the Lord." (KJV)

Ephesians 6:4 "And you, fathers, do not be irritating your children, but go on bringing them up in the discipline and mental-regulating of Jehovah." (NWT)

The Orwellian overtones regarding mental-regulating are sinister when put into the context of the Watchtower Society's demand for conformity.

The Watchtower Society, of course, paints this process in quite a different light. The Society points to the unity achieved by their members throughout the earth. Much is made of the fact that wherever Jehovah's Witnesses are to be found, the same doctrines and practices can be observed within their association. They are fond of quoting the Apostle Paul's words from his first letter to the Christians in Corinth, chapter one and verse ten:

"Now I exhort you, brethren, by the name of our Lord Jesus Christ, that you all agree, and there be no divisions among you, but you be made complete in the same mind and in the same judgement." (NAB)

This verse, declares the Watchtower Society, demonstrates that true Christians must all hold to the same interpretation of scripture. But when Paul counseled the Corinthian Christians to have the same mind and judgement, was he urging them to conform to the same precise scriptural interpretation as in the Society's explanation? The Complete Word Study Dictionary when discussing the Greek word for "mind" in this verse explains it to be:

"..mode of thinking and feeling, disposition, moral inclination, equivalent to the heart."[7] And again, when expanding on the word "judgement" in the same verse "With the meaning of bent, inclination, desire."[8]

The context shows that Paul was appealing to them to put aside attitudes and inclinations that were serving only to divide them. The unity that he urged was not of absolute conformity on interpretational issues, but as the Complete Word Study Dictionary makes clear, was a unity of purpose, of disposition, a common orientation toward Christ.

Nevertheless, the committed Witness will now be prepared to stake her life on the correctness of Watchtower Society doctrine as we have seen. Matters of conscience or preference are now handed over for the Society's arbitration as the following published questions from Witness readers demonstrate:

"Is it compatible with Bible principles for a Christian married couple to use birth control pills?"[9]

"Do Jehovah's Witnesses allow the use of autologous blood (auto transfusion), such as by having their own blood stored and later put back into them?"[10]

"Is it appropriate for a Christian to go hunting or fishing?"[11]

"Should a Christian avoid coffee and tea because they contain the addictive drug caffeine?"[12]

The very fact that these questions appear in the Watchtower indicates the extent to which the Witnesses have given the organisation authority. The Watchtower Society's direction impinges upon every aspect of its members' lives, including those of a very personal nature. The Society takes it upon itself to prohibit such things as oral and anal sex, sexual relations during menstruation, and masturbation.

Lest anyone think that these are suggestions only, individual married Witness couples have been disfellowshiped for their private sexual practices.[13] As in previous discussions, the issue is not whether one finds these sexual practices acceptable or not, but one which recognises that these are individual choices which must not be the subject of any organisation's decree.

The organisation also dictates the dress and grooming of its members. Female Witnesses must not wear trousers when engaged in preaching or attending the meetings. Men must not wear jumpers in the door to door work but must wear a jacket and tie. Even on the hottest of summer nights, it is a brave Witness that would risk appearing on the platform to deliver his student talk in the Ministry School without his jacket.

Short, neat hair is, of course, mandatory. Moustaches, if tidy, are permissible, but in Australia, a male Witness with a beard will not be appointed to a position of responsibility within the congregation nor used in any capacity requiring his onstage presence at a convention. He will be viewed with suspicion if he does not remove it. Of course only the vaguest scriptural backing can be given in support of these restrictions but an individual complaining about them will be told that his attitude is poor.

When an individual tolerates and in fact invites this level of interference in their lives, they open themselves up to manipulation and exploitation. While it may be argued by the individual Witness that the Watchtower Society does not exploit its members, it is not healthy for the individuals involved to adopt an attitude that infers they need direction in every aspect of their lives. It does not equip them to deal with other organisations of the world that may seek to exploit their dependent thinking for dishonest gain. It also makes the individual subservient to the organisation in many ways and this is one reason why it is so difficult for Witnesses to leave the organisation and adjust to the real world.

Relying heavily on an organisation also builds within many a fear of leaving, of being on their own, an actual fear of freedom. In this way they remain victims. Psychiatrist M. Scott Peck summed up this situation with the following words:

"One of the roots of this "sense of impotence" in the majority of patients is some desire to partially or totally escape the pain of freedom, and, therefore some failure, partial or total, to accept responsibility for their problems and their lives. They feel impotent because they have, in fact, given their power away. Sooner or later, if they are to be healed, they must learn that the entirety of one's adult life is a series of personal choices, decisions. If they can accept this totally, then they become free people. To the extent that they do not accept this they will forever feel themselves victims."[14]

There is a sense, therefore, that the personal identity of the Witness is submerged in the process of belonging to a much larger organisation and submitting to its authority. This comfort of authority can hinder the true spiritual and emotional maturity of the individual.

It is this unhealthy convention of seeing everything through the eyes of the Watchtower Society that allows the Witnesses to tolerate the basic doctrine of the Society, that the vast majority must die in order for the few chosen ones to enjoy life in the manner they choose. I cannot help but see parallels with movements such as the Nazis of Germany in the 1930's who held that entire races of people had to be exterminated in order that their own philosophy might thrive. It is ironic that the Jehovah's Witnesses themselves were one group earmarked by Hitler himself for such extermination.

Excused from responsibility

It seems fair to say that all persons share the collective responsibility for the damage that mankind has caused the planet as well as the suffering brought through war, natural disasters and famine. The massive and international relief efforts that are mounted combined with the huge sums of money raised to assist the victims of suffering demonstrate the responsibility felt by many.

The Witnesses however, see themselves as part of a giant cosmic courtroom drama with God on the one hand and the Devil on the other. To them, all of the suffering in the world is as a result of the Devil's interference in the affairs of men, the only solution to which is God's own intervention. On the surface therefore, it would be logical to conclude that any individual or agency working to restore good conditions to mankind would have the backing of God. Not so to the Witness mind. The Witnesses see the efforts of man in this area as fruitless and only a partial solution to the problem as they expect God to take care of such matters.

Worse than this, they often see involvement in activities aimed at solving the world's problems as time wasting distractions and in fact a strategy of the Devil to keep good people busy so that they will not listen to the all important message that the Witnesses proclaim. This logic is so obviously puerile that I will not spend time upon it. The important point is that this reasoning effectively frees the Witnesses from responsibility toward such problems, and leaves their time free for the door to door preaching work. It is my experience that many Witnesses actually look down on those attempting to solve problems related to the earth's environment for example, seeing them as well intentioned but misguided dupes of the Devil.

This is not to say that the individual Witness does not care about the problems and sufferings of the ill-fated in the world, but to a large extent they simply remain neutral. This seems an unfavourable outcome of a Christian philosophy at this time when their efforts could be directed toward benefiting their fellow man in ways that count. The entire community and not just the individual is poorer for this.

End of the world mentality

It is enlightening to flip back through the pages of the Watchtower magazine over the last thirty years and note the language used to describe the impending world calamity prophesied by the Witnesses.

One can take a Watchtower from thirty years ago and find the same urgency implied in the text. Non time specific language such as "in the time remaining" and "threshold of the New World" will be seen throughout, just as is the case today. Accordingly, as was true thirty years ago, we see children leaving school and entering into full time preaching work without regard to the effect this will have on their career prospects. We see many Witnesses making no real provision for their old age as they never expect to see it. I am continually amazed by the capacity of some Witnesses to hold the view, year after year, that the world's end is only a matter of months away. Surely this is self deception on a grand scale, and yet the Witnesses' vehemence regarding the impending Armageddon seems undiminished through time.

I once asked my father how he felt about the end of the world, twenty years after he sold his house and gave up his job in expectation of it happening. His response was illuminating. Far from being discouraged he said "Ah yes, but it's so much closer now than before."

Many good men and women wither under the strain of keeping the schedule of meeting attendance and study prescribed by the Society and develop mental and physical illness. Witnesses are encouraged to live with a sense of urgency as if they are in the midst of a crisis, but not many can keep this pace over a long period.

Families too are often neglected while parents are busy spending time in religious pursuits. Many wives are exiled into loneliness as their husbands spend countless evenings working on congregation problems. Children must be patient because there is often little time left over in many families for outings and picnics.

From infancy Witness children attend the meetings with their parents. Even when tiny, they must not be given toys to play with because their attention should be on the program. As soon as they are able, they will begin presenting literature from door to door. It is not at all uncommon to see children as young as ten and twelve knocking on doors with the Watchtower magazine and talking about the end of this wicked world. It seems to me a very sad thing that these children grow up with this doom and gloom outlook on life.

Mistrust of authority

Another undesirable outcome of the Witnesses' world view is their distrust, not only of those in authority, but of the authority itself. For example, Scientific knowledge often contradicts their view of the Genesis account of creation as we've seen. To counteract this, the Watchtower Society is fond of pointing out the mistakes of science in an effort to undermine its credibility. They are wont to put quotes around the words science and scientist as a way of presenting them to the Witnesses as sort of atheistic pseudo-wise men.

Among many Witnesses this suspicious attitude extends to school teachers, doctors and academics generally. It is no surprise then, that alternative medical practitioners have a lucrative business with the Witnesses as they appear to use folk medicine and natural therapies instead of the more traditional methods inspired by "worldly" knowledge.

While a certain amount of caution and scepticism is undoubtedly useful to the individual, it is my experience that the Witnesses as a group seem to raise this suspicion to a level that is not functional but merely causes them to become intolerant of others.

It is my view that many Bible principles by which

the Witnesses claim to be guided are sound and may serve to build good character. The Watchtower Society however, takes these fundamentals and wraps them up in so much theological baggage that the end result is neither palatable nor healthy for the individual.

I am reminded of the Pharisees of the first century. Their very name means "separated ones." This group saw the approach to God existing through obedience to the law. They took the simple laws of the Bible such as the instruction regarding the Sabbath day and built volumes of minor regulations around it until every last action was covered by legislation.

This placed an enormous and unnecessary burden on the people. The Pharisees opposed Jesus because he pointed out the folly of their ways. In many respects we seem to have come full circle, as now, to be acceptable to God, the Watchtower Society insists, we have to observe not only what the Bible says, but also the myriad of additional requirements laid down by the Society. It seems, in this matter at least, that history does indeed repeat itself and man does not profit from its passing.

The Heart of The Matter

"Be thankful that your lot has fallen
on times when, though there may be
many evil tongues and exasperated
spirits, there are none who have fire
and fagot at command."

Robert Southey

One of the main reasons why Jehovah's Witnesses
as a group continue to survive and indeed increase in
numbers, is the collective devotion shown by Witness
members toward their organisation. As we have seen,
the organisation is endowed with massive authority
both in areas of private life as well as scriptural
exposition. But the question to which most Witnesses
give no attention is: What actually is the organisation?
In this chapter I will attempt to answer that question
and give my view of the position that such an

organisation should occupy in the life of a Christian.

It was well said by Alexander Herzen, a Russian journalist and political thinker:

"All religions have based morality on obedience, that is to say, on voluntary slavery. That is why they have always been more pernicious than any political organisation. For the latter makes use of violence, the former - of the corruption of the will."[1]

Christianity has always been concerned with morality. The Bible sets out its own brand of morality, even in as simple a form as the Ten Commandments, and men and women for thousands of years have tried to espouse those standards. What we observe in the Watchtower Society however, is an organisation which goes beyond what is written in scripture and imposes its own brand of morality on its members. As we have seen, this effectively regulates the way they think, speak, and act in all facets of life including the forfeiture of that life before disobedience to the organisation's tenets. No organisation should exercise such a level of control over an individual, it is unhealthy for the individual themselves as well as society as a whole.

As long as the Witnesses perceive the organisation to be spirit directed by God, they will continue to empower it in this fashion. To the extent that they refuse to critically evaluate the message coming from the organisation, they will not be able to see through its diaphanous principles. But let us return to the original question "what is the organisation?"

Jehovah's Witnesses are told that God has always used an organisation to communicate his will to his people on earth.[2] A false dilemma is created in their minds, perpetrated by the Watchtower Society's literature, that there must be only one organisation with the "truth" from God and thus all others by definition are false. Once this frame of mind is established and the individual is convinced that the Watchtower Society is that "true" organisation, her thinking loses its objectivity and new information from the organisation is analysed in the context of "revealed truth" rather than on its own merits.

To question the organisation is to question God. To lack faith in the organisation is to lack faith in God. To break the rules of the organisation invites the sanctions spelled out in the Bible for those who transgress God's law. The organisation is seen to illuminate the law of God and show its application in the lives of individual Christians.

But let us question the very assumption that underpins this whole procedure: Has God always communicated his will through an organisation? This is a pivotal issue, for without divine backing for its organisation, the Watchtower Society's theology collapses like a house of cards.

From the beginning of the Bible record, the scriptures reveal that God communicated to and through *individuals*. We see God speaking directly with Adam, the first man of the Bible. Adam's son Cain was directly addressed by God. Noah was said to be a righteous man (not part of an approved organisation) before God. The righteousness of his sons and their wives as well as Noah's own wife, all of whom are said to have survived the flood, is not even mentioned. The early part of the Old Testament is a record of God's dealings with faithful individuals such as Abraham, Joseph, Moses and others.

As time progressed, the entire nation of Israel comprised God's people according to the biblical record. But was this an organisation after the fashion of the Watchtower Society today? No, it was a patriarchy, a large family organised along family lines. Moses was a mediator, a "channel" through which God addressed the nation, but it was still a family. The Elders and "chieftains" were related to those over whom they held authority. The entire nation was divided into "tribes" based on bloodlines.

In fact it was only when the people actually craved a King to rule over them after the pattern of the nations around them that things started to deteriorate. The nation was torn in two after only a brief history with organised Kingship.

When God wanted to communicate or correct his large Israelite family, he used prophets. These prophets were appointed by God and not some earthly organisation holding forth qualifications to be met. Because of this fact, Israel had to be given a threefold test to apply to the prophet's utterance to determine whether the prophet spoke in harmony with God's will or not.[3] Clearly, Israel did not constitute an organisation in the form of the Watchtower Society.

In Jesus' day, was there a central organisation from which Christians received direction? The Watchtower Society make much of the body of Elders in the first century congregation of Jerusalem, assigning them the position of Governing Body, on which they model their own executive council. A careful examination of the scriptures shows that rather than an organisation that was somehow led collectively by God, individuals such as Paul were used to correct the thinking of some on issues related to the law of Moses and its applicability to the Gentile Christians.[4]

Throughout the New Testament, the emphasis is on individuals accepting Christ as their savior. Individuals who converted to Christianity such as Cornelius and the Ethiopian on the road to Gaza were simply lead to Christ for direction, not to an organisation of any sort. Although the Bible chronicles the actions of many faithful individuals, it in no way endorses an organisation with the authority over individuals held by the Watchtower Society.

Of course one of the reasons that organisations are formed is that they can accomplish more than can one individual. So often an organisation founded to further a noble or worthy cause becomes a victim of its own momentum and proceeds to enslave the very members it was established to liberate. The Watchtower Society promises a release from "false religious belief" and then goes on to bind the new convert with as many if not more of it's own regulations, with little real foundation other than its personal claim of divine backing.

The Witnesses themselves point to the need for the organisation in order to accomplish the global preaching effort which they see as their primary work. Much is made of the fact that the Witnesses are active in over 200 countries and islands of the sea. The whole story, however, is rather different. Although in many Western countries Jehovah's Witnesses are conspicuous in their house to house work, in lands such as China, India and Pakistan, which together comprise more than one third of all people living on the earth, the Witnesses are relatively silent. To these areas we may add hundreds of millions of individuals in many of the predominantly Muslim countries of the world. This is not to say that the Witnesses are inactive in these places, but their impact is inconsequential due to the enormous Witness to population ratio.

Even where the Witnesses call frequently in lands such as the United States, Great Britain and Australia, the population is largely ignorant of the Watchtower Society's message. To assume that individual householders are making a life or death decision based on a few-minute doorstep sermon is ludicrous.

Neither can we believe the claim of the Witnesses that God's imprimatur must be with their organisation as evidenced by its numerical growth. Other religious organisations that had their start in the United States during the nineteenth century such as the Seventh Day Adventists and Mormons show similar rates of growth.

Despite this, the Watchtower Society makes pretentious claims on behalf of its members such as this extract from the Watchtower of March 15 1986:

"Only in the spiritual paradise, among Jehovah's Witnesses, can we find the self-sacrificing love Jesus said would identify his true disciples (John 13:34, 35)... Because they are taught by God, Jehovah's Witnesses really produce the fruits of Christianity in their lives... Only they have an organisation that completely abides by what God's word has to say on sexual immorality, abortions, drunkenness, stealing, idolatry, racial prejudice, and other worldly pursuits and practices. And they alone are the ones obeying the command to preach the good news of Jehovah's Kingdom. (Matthew 24:14) God's own Word unquestionably points to Jehovah's Witnesses as the one organised people that have his blessing."[5]

It may be "unquestionable" to the Watchtower Society, but such a smug, arrogant attitude is in fact a recipe for religious intolerance. It is no surprise, fed with such a diet of propaganda, that the Witnesses can see no good in any other religious organisation. In fact, in holding to this perspective, they have over time actually turned through one hundred and eight degrees.

It was their founder Charles Russell who claimed in the March 1883 edition of the Watchtower that the whole philosophy of an organisation was "worldly" and a clear act of sectarianism. Neither would he or his followers be known by any name other than "Christians."[6] One can only speculate about what Russell would have made of the Watchtower Society today.

The individual members of the Watchtower Society may not care to admit it, but their organisation bears all the hallmarks of the religious cults in our 20th century. Far from being "unique" or "the only true faith" the Witnesses share many identifying marks with the religious organisations that they condemn.

Anthony Hoekema, a well respected author on the

topic of unconventional religious groups, sets out five distinguishing characteristics in identifying a cult.[7] From our discussion thus far, it should be obvious that Jehovah's Witnesses posses every one.

1. An extra scriptural Authority

This is easily identifiable in the Watchtower Society itself which claims that a true understanding of scripture can only be found through its interpretation. The Society's "law" becomes as binding as the Bible's

2. The denial of justification by grace alone

Instead of salvation through God's gift, Witnesses must adhere to certain conditions and requirements such as door to door preaching to "earn" such salvation. Although lip service is rendered to the concept of grace, the works of each individual Christian are the primary focus.

3. The devaluation of Christ

Within the Witness community, the emphasis is shifted from Christ to God. Christ is held as inferior to God. His sacrifice does not save mankind, it merely enables them to be saved. Those who will survive Armageddon must prove themselves obedient to the laws of God and thus save themselves. "Believe on the Lord" is understood to be only the beginning, not the end.

4. The group as the exclusive community of the saved

As the cult absolutises itself as the only true community of God's people, (true in the case of the Watchtower Society) it must concentrate on showing all other faiths to be false and instruments of the devil. Only those responding positively to the message of the Watchtower Society will be saved at Armageddon.

5. The groups central role in eschatology

The cult sees itself as being formed by God for some special work at the end of the age, the climax of man's affairs. We see this clearly in the Watchtower Society and the preaching work that constitutes its main activity. The Witnesses believe that their organisation was formed toward the end of the 19th century to fill a need that God had for preachers of the Good News.

Rather than uniqueness, these traits confer upon Jehovah's Witnesses many similarities with other unconventional religious groups throughout the earth. What the Witnesses offer to people differs only in flavour not in substance from these other groups.

What, then, will be the future of the Jehovah's Witnesses? It appears to me that they will have to re-jig their major doctrinal position regarding 1914 in the near future. No doubt this will cost them many members as did the 1975 debacle. I don't doubt, however, that the organisation will continue to exist for there will always be vulnerable people and those who prefer a world of black and white in which to operate, even if that world is artificial. The organisation, having almost eight million members, also has a great deal of momentum and no doubt this energy will carry them forward for many years to come.

My own involvement with them has taught me a great deal. I have learned how easy it is to lose one's perspective and objectivity. As time progresses I am able to see the organisation for what it is, just another cult selling religious elitism and bigotry as freedom. I have seen many of its members diminished as individuals through their obedience to the Watchtower Society's dogma while at the same time having their personalities augmented by the application of Christian principles over which mercifully, the Society does not hold exclusive franchise. I have also learned that all individuals must take responsibility for their own thoughts and convictions, and that everyone is impoverished when free debate is squashed.

Although I know in my heart that I will never again be part of any organisation or society that crushes the human spirit, I would not want to see the organisation of the Witnesses oppressed. My hope is that, as time advances, people will gain increasing access to information which will empower them to make sound decisions regarding their religious future. If an individual wishes to join the Jehovah's Witnesses or the Scientologists or the Mormons, let her do so with the full knowledge and understanding of what these organisations offer and expect. Unfortunately, I suspect that this will never fully be the case and that, as with all freedoms, religious freedom comes at a price.

It is also my view that organisations which employ comparable methods such as discouraging independent thinking, not tolerating dissent, separating their members socially and intellectually from the rest of the community, claiming to have the ultimate authority or special revelation, and so on, can be plotted along a horizontal line. At the far right of this line we find Jim Jones and the People's Temple together with David Koresh and other sociopaths. The Watchtower Society also exists on this same line, a long way to the left of the Jonestown massacre but much farther right than other groups. I understand that this may be offensive to many Witnesses but to my mind all of these organisations are just variations on the same theme, producing in their followers similar results which differ in degree rather than in nature.

One of the many challenges facing society today is to determine how far religious toleration should be extended to organisations that damage or put at risk the lives of their adherents. To what extent should people be protected from themselves? I don't presume to have the answers, but it is my sincere hope that anyone reading this book will think seriously about where they desire to place themselves along the line that begins with the Sermon on the Mount and ends with religious monomania.

Conclusion

The last few years of my life have been accompanied by great upheaval and change. This is, of course, not uniquely my experience for many people make fundamental changes to their lives and still more have change inflicted upon them. Perhaps what is important is not the magnitude of the change but the direction our lives take as we emerge from the process.

It was Leo Tolstoy that said:

"The changes in our life must come from the impossibility to live otherwise than according to the demands of our conscience... not from our mental resolution to try a new form of life."

In many ways this sums up my feelings after the disentanglement from my former life. I feel deeply the sense of loss that results from damage to once cherished relationships as well as the pain that my actions have caused others. But there is also a sense of a new beginning, a chance to be honest and open about who I am and what I believe, without looking over my shoulder or seeking approval from another.

I no longer feel that I am being carried along by a wave of blind credulity which inevitably must exhaust itself on the shore of disappointment. My life is now headed in a different direction, one which guarantees more questions than answers, but a direction that is determined by me alone.

The future holds many challenges, not the least of which is developing new friends and opening my eyes to the breadth and complexity of the real world. I am confident, however, that in this I will be successful and indeed have already made good progress. I am also conscious of the fact that my thinking has been shaped by twenty five years of association with the Watchtower Society and I need to be vigilant not to fall back on this pattern when confronted with new situations or ideas. This is at once both frightening and liberating. I am no longer plagued by thoughts of suicide and that period of my life seems a long way off, almost as if it was confided to me by a close friend, and not my own experience at all.

My thoughts of the future are encapsulated by the words of Robert Frost:

The woods are lovely, dark and deep.

But I have promises to keep,

And miles to go before I sleep.

Afterward

It is an interesting experience to read something written almost twenty years ago and at a significant period in one's life. To be brutally honest, my overwhelming response was cringing embarrassment. Embarrassment that I actually persevered in this organisation for as long as I did. Embarrassment that I actually professed a belief to other people in such puerile drivel. And most of all, shame that some individuals embraced what I told them and joined the organisation themselves.

I'm angry too when I think back to the feelings I had of being trapped when in fact the solution was in my hands all along. It's hard for me now to relate to the person I was twenty years ago. It feels like someone else's story.

With the benefit of two decades of hindsight I now see the Watchtower Society in a context that I really just couldn't acknowledge for some time. In fact, I almost gave up on making this book available to others as it felt so incredibly stupid to be refuting such inane and obviously senseless doctrine that didn't deserve my or anyone else's time. I guess what this demonstrates is the power over people that such organisations can wield – particularly people who are raised knowing little else.

I have no real desire to dissuade current Jehovah's Witnesses from their faith but I do hope that this small book will make any prospective converts think twice about joining in the first place. The Watchtower Society makes their organisation an easy and welcoming place to join but a very difficult place to leave.

As far as God is concerned, my thoughts are clear now. I am infinitely more comfortable as an atheist than I ever was as a Christian. Where once I had doubt, now I have certainty. This is not to say that the experience does not still affect me; we are all shaped by our journey through life and I still have bad dreams associated with the Watchtower Society and door knocking. The Yarra Valley area of Melbourne where I lived as part of the Jehovah's Witness community will be forever ruined for me. To this day I can't drive through that area without feelings of unease.

I said earlier that my father sold our house in 1972 because he believed the world would end soon. He didn't only sell the house, he also gave up his job and intended to live on the proceeds of the sale. The house was sold to an investor and immediately rented back, my father handing over two years advance rent.

Astute readers will notice that two years advance rent from 1972 is actually less than what will be required if the world is to end in 1975. So certain was my father of the Watchtower Society's teaching that he couldn't even imagine the world would last to 1975. In his estimation the two years advance rent was more than enough to get us into the new world he'd been promised.

At the time the ownership of our family home was being handed to a stranger, I was a fourteen year old schoolboy. My father saw absolutely no point in schoolwork and considering that the world's end was imminent, encouraged me to take it easy and to leave school as soon as I could legally do so. Like many boys of my age I didn't need to be told twice and so left on my fifteenth birthday. Not the smartest decision I have ever made but my father was not alone in taking these drastic steps and dragging his family along with him.

When the world inconveniently refused to end, my parents moved into rental accommodation before purchasing a mobile home and living on our property for ten years while they restored their financial position. Later I remarried, went back to school and after many years completed a Masters Degree at Monash University. Now, my life is happy, fulfilling and as I move closer to sixty than fifty, increasingly content.

As the restoration of this book was triggered by the death of my father, I should say something of his recent years too.

My father was one of the few Jehovah's Witnesses that I knew that had absolutely no doubts about Watchtower Society doctrine. He believed absolutely in the concept of an Armageddon that would wipe the world clean to be subsequently enjoyed by Jehovah's Witnesses alone. Only two weeks before he died, he harangued me with a question on his favorite topic – the United Nations and its role in triggering the end of the world.

He wanted me to promise him that when the U.N. formally banned religion throughout the world, I would recognise the sign for what it was and essentially scurry back to the protection of the Watchtower Society. I patiently explained that even if such an unlikely scenario should eventuate, I would rather cast my lot among the dead than live within world built on the deaths of billions of people. As I've said before, the obscene parallel to Nazi Germany is too obvious. I'm not sure that he believed me.

In his final years, the doctrine of the Watchtower Society proved to be a double edged sword for my father. After my mother died in November 2009, he lost his joy in life. Where many people find comfort in their faith at such times, my father became trapped in a kind of waiting room. He was certain that, as believed by all Jehovah's Witnesses, my mother would not be in heaven but would receive a resurrection back to life on earth. In anticipation of this he kept her things and their house in immaculate condition, even vacuuming the carpets daily as had been her custom. He believed with total certainty that one day she would walk through the front door, and he did everything within his power to ensure things were just as she left them.

In the meantime he couldn't seem to move forward as he waited for her return. Every time some violence or civil strife erupted somewhere in the world, he would eagerly anticipate this event being the trigger for the UN to play its part in the role that the

Watchtower Society has cast for it - the first step in the process that results in the Armageddon conceived by the Witnesses. Of course it never happened. In the end the waiting and the loneliness became too much and he chose to end his life.

He died as he lived – calling things as he saw them without fear or favour. I didn't agree with most of what he believed but I respected his principled stand and his honesty. I have no doubt that he will never see my mother again but at least he misses her no longer.

Finally, a few words about the contents of this book.

I should say at this point that it is very unlikely that Jehovah's Witnesses will actually read this book. In fact they are routinely encouraged to see material such as this as evil and my promulgation of it as unforgiveable. I don't care too much about that. I don't consider myself to be evil and this book is simply my opinion on a range of matters but that's not how it will be received. The only context in which what I've written is even controversial is one where free and independent thinking is suppressed.

I'm also not even remotely interested in a crusade against existing members of the Jehovah's Witnesses movement. Life is too short to be campaigning in some sort of anti Watchtower battle. Besides, people are entitled to hold whatever religious beliefs they choose, regardless of how much sense it makes to others. If anyone reading this book is a part of such an anti Witness movement, please don't ask me to join. I will not.

Having said this, I don't think that the community is advantaged by having groups of people living in a detached fantasy world of their own making. Neither is it good for their own mental health to live constantly with the expectation that, any day now, all of their neighbours will be killed so they can have this planet to themselves. It also happens to be a reprehensible and shameful doctrine.

So, given that existing Witnesses will likely not be exposed to the contents within these pages, the Watchtower Society will be concerned that this book may dissuade potential recruits from accepting the Jehovah's Witness faith. In response I can only say that I certainly hope it does. If only one person is moved to close the door and not become involved because of what I've written, it will have been well worth the effort.

If you are thinking of joining the Witnesses because they seem like good decent folk, they are. But what they believe is not good and it's not correct and it's not even Christian in my opinion. And I've seen it up close. Don't join.

References

Chapter one – Where it began

1. *Jehovah's Witnesses, Proclaimers of God's Kingdom*, Watchtower Bible and Tract Society 1983, p. 725

2. Walter Martin & Norman Klann, *Jehovah of the Watchtower*, Bethany House Publishers p. 13

3. Robert U. Finnerty, *Jehovah's Witnesses on Trial*, Presbyterian and Reformed Publishing Company p. 12

4. Anthony A. Hokema, *The Four Major Cults*, WM. B. Eerdmans Publishing Co. p. 225

5. Walter Martin & Norman Klann, *Jehovah of the Watchtower*, Bethany House Publishers p. 13

6. *Watchtower* December 1 1916, Watchtower Bible and Tract Society p. 357 *

7. Anthony A. Hokema, *The Four Major Cults*, WM. B. Eerdmans Publishing Co. p. 228

8. Raymond Franz, *Crisis of Conscience*, Commentary Press p. 55

9. Isaiah 43:10

10. Anthony A. Hokema, *The Four Major Cults*, WM. B. Eerdmans Publishing Co. p. 231 & Duane Magnani, *The Watchtower Files*, Bethany House Publishers p. 58

11. Raymond Franz, *Crisis of Conscience*, Commentary Press p. 50

12. Robert M. Bowman jr., *Understanding Jehovah's Witnesses*, Baker Book House p. 63

13. Compton's Interactive Encyclopedia, Compton's NewMedia Inc.

14. David A. Reed, *Jehovah's Witness Literature*, Baker Book House p. 9

15. *Jehovah's Witnesses, Proclaimers of God's Kingdom*, Watchtower Bible and Tract Society 1983, p. 351

16. *Mankind's Search for God*, Watchtower Bible and Tract Society p. 360-362

17. *Ibid.*, p. 360

18. *Ibid.*, p. 362-363

19. Consider any Index to Watchtower Society publications

20. *Our Kingdom Ministry*, Watchtower Bible and Tract Society, p. 3

* *"Watchtower Bible and Tract Society" is used throughout to denote the publisher of Watchtower literature. Although in the past this legal entity has existed under different names such as the "People's Pulpit Association," it is best known under its current name and hence this is how I will refer to it.*

21. Raymond Franz, *Crisis of Conscience*, Commentary Press p. 243

22. *Jehovah's Witnesses, Proclaimers of God's Kingdom*, Watchtower Bible and Tract Society 1983, p. 299

23. *Jehovah's Witnesses, Proclaimers of God's Kingdom*,

Watchtower Bible and Tract Society 1983, p. 717

24. *Jehovah's Witnesses, Proclaimers of God's Kingdom*, Watchtower Bible and Tract Society 1983, p. 320-321

Chapter two – Why does it work ?

1. For example, see "Watching the World", a two page feature in every issue of *Awake!* Magazine

2. *Watchtower*, April 1 1986, Watchtower Bible and Tract Society, p.51

3. Adolf Hitler, *Mein Kampf*, Vol 1 ch. 6

4. *Let Your Kingdom Come*, Watchtower Bible and Tract Society, p. 182-183

5. *Watchtower* September 1 1990, Watchtower Bible and Tract Society p. 30

6. *Our Kingdom Ministry* April 1991, Watchtower Bible and Tract Society, p. 8

7. M. Scott Peck, *The Road Less Travelled*, Simon and Schuster 1978, p.42

8. *Watchtower* July 15 1989, Watchtower Bible and Tract Society, p. 11-12

9. *Watchtower* December 1 1976,Watchtower Bible and Tract Society, p. 725-730

10. Walter Martin & Norman Klann, *Jehovah of the Watchtower*, Bethany House Publishers 1974, p.92-93

11. *Mankind's Search for God*, Watchtower Bible and Tract Society p. 360

12. For example, *Life – How did it get here? By evolution or by creation?*, Watchtower   Bible and Tract Society, p. 105-107

13. *Holman Bible Dictionary*, Holman Bible Publishers, p. 1429

14. Raymond Franz, *Crisis of Conscience*, Commentary Press p. 50

15. Robert H. Countess, *The Jehovah's Witnesses' New Testament*, Presbyterian and Reformed Publishing Co., p. 93

16. Dr. William Barclay, The Expository Times Nov. 1953, cited by William I. Cetnar, *Questions for Jehovah's Witnesses*, p. 55

17. W.E. Vine, *Vines Expository Dictionary of New Testament Words*, Macdonald Publishing Company, p. 638

18. *Ibid.*, p. 698

19. *Mankind's Search for God*, Watchtower Bible and Tract Society p. 356-357

20. *Watchtower* March 1 1991, Watchtower Bible and Tract Society, p. 28

21. Robert H. Countess, *The Jehovah's Witnesses' New Testament*, Presbyterian and Reformed Publishing Co., p. 91

22. Robert M. Bowman jr., *Jehovah's Witnesses, Jesus Christ, and the Gospel of John*, Baker Book House

23. David A. Reed, *Jehovah's Witnesses answered verse by verse*, Baker Book House, p. 21.

Chapter three – Let thy Kingdom come

1. *Holman Bible Dictionary*, Holman Bible Publishers, p. 1012

2. *Let Your Kingdom Come*, Watchtower Bible and Tract Society, p. 134

3. *Ibid.*, p.138-139

4. W.E.Vine, *Vine's Expository Dictionary of New Testament Words*, Macdonald Publishing Company, p.1161

5. Revelation 12:1-6

6. *Let Your Kingdom Come*, Watchtower Bible and

Tract Society, p. 137

7. J.M. Roberts, *History of the World*, Helicon Publishing Ltd, p. 206-207

8. *Ibid.*, p.136-137

9. Raymond Franz, *Crisis of Conscience*, Commentary Press p. 25-26

10. This has been acknowledged many times by the Watchtower Society and is obvious form historical records.

11. Numbers 14:34 – *Let Your Kingdom Come*, Watchtower Bible and Tract Society,   p. 136-137

12. Raymond Franz, *Crisis of Conscience*, Commentary Press p. 142-147

13. *The Time is at Hand*, 1889 edition, Watchtower Bible and Tract Society, p.77

14. Spiros Zodhiates, *The Complete Word Study Dictionary – New Testament*, AMG   Publishers   p. 1123

15. *Mankind's Search for God*, Watchtower Bible and Tract Society p. 368

16. *Watchtower* January 1 1924, Watchtower Bible and Tract Society, p. 5

17. *The Finished Mystery*, Watchtower Bible and Tract Society, p. 485

18. *The Finished Mystery*, Watchtower Bible and Tract Society, p. 258

19. *Millions Now Living Will Never Die*, Watchtower Bible and Tract Society, p. 90

20. *Watchtower* December 15 1941, Watchtower Bible and Tract Society, p. 372

21. *Ibid.*, p.377

22. *Judge Rutherford Uncovers Fifth Column*, Watchtower Bible and Tract Society, p.   15

23. *Watchtower* September 15 1941, Watchtower Bible

and Tract Society, p. 288

24. W.A. Elwell, *Evangelical Dictionary of Theology*, Baker Book House, p. 391

25. *Life Everlasting in Freedom of The Sons of God*, Watchtower Bible and Tract Society, p. 29-30

26. *Kingdom Ministry* May 1974, Watchtower Bible and Tract Society,

27. *Watchtower* May 1 1968, Watchtower Bible and Tract Society, p. 272

28. *Watchtower* August 15 1968, Watchtower Bible and Tract Society, p.

29. *Watchtower* July 15 1976, Watchtower Bible and Tract Society, p. 432

30. Genesis 2:23

31. *Watchtower* July 15 1976, Watchtower Bible and Tract Society, p. 441

32. David A. Reed, *Jehovah's Witness Literature*, Baker Book House p. 172-173

33. Matthew 24, Luke 21

34. Matthew 24:4-51

35. *Longman Illustrated Encyclopedia of World History*, Ivy Leaf Publishers, p. 490

36. *Let Your Kingdom Come*, Watchtower Bible and Tract Society, p. 106-107

37. *Ibid.*, p. 112-115

38. Luke 21:32

39. *Let Your Kingdom Come*, Watchtower Bible and Tract Society, p. 140

40. Luke 21:32 *New World Translation*, Watchtower Bible and Tract Society

41. *Awake* October 8 1968, Watchtower Bible and Tract Society, p. 13

42. *Watchtower* October 15 1980, Watchtower Bible and Tract Society, p. 31

43. *Watchtower* May 15 1984, Watchtower Bible and Tract Society, p. 5

44. I Thessalonians 5:3 *New World Translation*, Watchtower Bible and Tract Society

45. Matthew 24:15 *New World Translation*, Watchtower Bible and Tract Society

46. *Mankind's Search for God*, Watchtower Bible and Tract Society p. 370

47. Revelation 20:7

48. Revelation 20:8a

49. Revelation 20:8b

Chapter four – An exclusive club

1. *Mankind's Search for God*, Watchtower Bible and Tract Society p. 369

2. *Let Your Kingdom Come*, Watchtower Bible and Tract Society, p. 164

3. *Ibid.*, p. 167

4. *Ibid.*, p. 166

5. *Mankind's Search for God*, Watchtower Bible and Tract Society p. 377

6. *Holman Bible Dictionary*, Holman Bible Publishers, p. 753

7. B.M. Metzger & M.D. Coogan, *The Oxford Companion to the Bible*, Oxford University Press, p. 343

8. Robert H. Countess, *The Jehovah's Witnesses' New Testament*, Presbyterian and Reformed Publishing Co., p. 39-40

9. For example, The Society of Friends (Quakers)

10. *Watchtower* April 15 1903, Watchtower Bible and Tract Society, p. 120

11. *Watchtower* February 15 1951, Watchtower Bible and Tract Society, p. 73

12. Anthony A. Hokema, *The Four Major Cults*, WM. B. Eerdmans Publishing Co.

p.252

13. *Jehovah's Witnesses, Proclaimers of God's Kingdom*, Watchtower Bible and Tract Society 1983, p. 144

14. Genesis 1:19 (KJV)

15. Exodus 20:8-11

16. *Let Your Kingdom Come*, Watchtower Bible and Tract Society, p. 80

17. Raymond Franz, *In Search of Christian Freedom*, Commentary Press, p. 598

18.

19. *Let Your Kingdom Come*, Watchtower Bible and Tract Society, p. 8-9

20. W.A. Elwell, *Evangelical Dictionary of Theology*, Baker Book House, p. 611

21. Anthony A. Hokema, *The Four Major Cults*, WM. B. Eerdmans Publishing Co.

p.266

22. *Watchtower* March 1 1923, Watchtower Bible and Tract Society, p. 68

23. *Watchtower* September 15 1922, Watchtower Bible and Tract Society, p. 279

24. C.T. Russell, *Thy Kingdom Come*, Watchtower Bible and Tract Society, p.314

25. *Watchtower* June 15 1922, Watchtower Bible and Tract Society, p. 187

26. *Watchtower* November 15 1928, Watchtower Bible and Tract Society, p. 341

27. *Ibid.*, p. 344

28. C.T. Russell*Thy Kingdom Come*, Watchtower Bible and Tract Society, p.327

29. *Watchtower* November 15 1953, Watchtower Bible and Tract Society, p. 703

30. C.T. Russell*The Finished Mystery*, Watchtower Bible and Tract Society, 85

31. Dumas Malone, *Dictionary of American Biography vol VIII*, Charles Scribner's
    Sons, p. 240
32. *Ibid.*, p. 240
33. *Watchtower* March 1 1923, Watchtower Bible and Tract Society, p. 71
34. Supreme court, Moyle v Franz *et al.*,cited in David A. Reed, *Jehovah's Witness Literature*, Baker Book House, p. 19
35. A.H. MacMillan, *Faith on the March*, Englewood Cliffs: Prentice Hall, p.79
36. A.H. MacMillan, *Faith on the March*, p. 152, cited in Raymond Franz, *Crisis of Conscience*, Commentary Press p. 59
37. Raymond Franz, *Crisis of Conscience*, Commentary Press p. 61
38. John F. Walvoord & Roy B. Zuck, *The Bible Knowledge Commentary Vol I*, Victor books 1985, p.914
39. *Matthew Henry's Commentary on the Whole Bible*, Vol III, Hendrickson Publishers 1991, p.667
40. *Jehovah's Witnesses, Proclaimers of God's Kingdom*, Watchtower Bible and Tract Society 1983, p. 144-145

Chapter five – The trouble with science

1.   For example, see "Watching the World", a two page feature in every issue of *Awake!* Magazine
2.   *The Bible, God's word or man's*, Watchtower Bible and Tract Society 1989, p.24

3. Robert Shapiro, *Origins,* Penguin Books, p. 80

4. Duane T. Gish and Richard B. Bliss. Summary of scientific evidence for creation (parts IV-VII). ICR Impact Series, no 96 p. iii cited in *Scientists Confront Creationism*, Penguin Books, p. 51

5. *Life-How did it get here? By evolution or creation?*, Watchtower Bible and Tract Society, p. 26

6. *Ibid.,* p. 27

7. *Is The Bible Really The Word of God?*, Watchtower Bible and Tract Society, p. 23- 25

8. Isaac Asimov, quoted in Douglas J. Futuyma, *Science on Trial – The Case for Evolution,* Pantheon Books, p. 175

9. *Life-How did it get here? By evolution or creation?*, Watchtower Bible and Tract Society, p. 37

10. Genesis 3:1 (NAB)

11. *Comptons Interactive Encyclopedia,* Comptons Newmedia Inc., 1993,1994

12. Genesis 6:13 (NAB)

13. *Is The Bible Really The Word of God?*, Watchtower Bible and Tract Society, p. 42

14. *The Bible, God's word or man's,* Watchtower Bible and Tract Society 1989, p.110- 111

15. Lawrie R. Godfrey, *Scientists Confront Creationism,* Penguin Books, p. 288

16. L.G. Soroka and C.L. Nelson, Physical constraints on the Noachian deluge. *Journal of Geological Education* 31: 134-139. Cited in D.R. Selkirk and F.J. Burrows, *Confronting Creationism: Defending Darwin,* The New South Wales University Press, p. 131

17. *Ibid.,* p. 132

18. *Ibid.,* p. 132

19. *Is The Bible Really The Word of God?*, Watchtower Bible and Tract Society, p. 42

20. *Life-How did it get here? By evolution or creation?*, Watchtower Bible and Tract Society, p. 35-36

21. *Is The Bible Really The Word of God?*, Watchtower Bible and Tract Society, p. 43

22. Richard Dawkins, *The Blind Watchmaker*, Penguin Books, p. 79

23. *Life-How did it get here? By evolution or creation?*, Watchtower Bible and Tract Society, p. 15

24. Francis Hitching, *The Neck of the Giraffe or Where Darwin went wrong,* Pan Books, p. 12

25. *Life-How did it get here? By evolution or creation?*, Watchtower Bible and Tract Society, p. 23

26. *Life-How did it get here? By evolution or creation?*, Watchtower Bible and Tract Society, p. 18

27. Charles Darwin, *The Origin of Species*, Penguin Books, p. 217

28. *Ibid.*, p. 219

29. *Life-How did it get here? By evolution or creation?*, Watchtower Bible and Tract Society, p.79-80

30. Douglas J. Futuyma, *Science on Trial – The Case for Evolution*, Pantheon Books 1982, p. 188,189

31. *Ibid.*, p.189

32. D.R. Selkirk & F.J. Burrows, *Confronting Creationism: Defending Darwin*, The NSW University Press 1987, p. 79

33. Stephen Jay Gould, *The Panda's Thumb*, Penguin Books 1983, p.225

34. *Life-How did it get here? By evolution or creation?*, Watchtower Bible and Tract Society, p.97

35. Ian Plimer, *Telling Lies for God: Reason vs Creationism*, Random House 1994, p.27

36. *Life-How did it get here? By evolution or creation?*, Watchtower Bible and Tract Society, p. 94

37. Lawrie R. Godfrey, *Scientists Confront Creationism*,

Penguin Books, p. 251

38. *Life-How did it get here? By evolution or creation?*, Watchtower Bible and Tract Society, p.86

39. Donald C. Johanson & Maitland A. Edey, *Lucy – The Beginnings of Humankind*, Book Club Associates 1981, p.221

40. *Life-How did it get here? By evolution or creation?*, Watchtower Bible and Tract Society, p.90

41. *Ibid.*, p.90-91

42. *Ibid.*, p.4

43. Alan Rogerson, *Millions Now Living Will Never Die: A Study of Jehovah's Witnesses*, Constable, p. 116

Chapter six – A question of inerrancy

1. Judges 14:8-9
2. Judges 16:1
3. Judges 16:4-20
4. Judges 15:6
5. Judges 15:4+5
6. Judges 14:3+4
7. Matthew 24:37-39
8. *Jehovah's Witnesses, Proclaimers of God's Kingdom*, Watchtower Bible and Tract Society 1983, p. 704
9. *Ibid.*, p.709
10. John 3:16
11. Psalms 137:7-9
12. *Jehovah's Witnesses, Proclaimers of God's Kingdom*, Watchtower Bible and Tract Society 1983, p. 11
13. 1 Timothy 2:14
14. Deuteronomy 32:4

Chapter seven – Separate from the world

1. *Jehovah's Witnesses, Proclaimers of God's Kingdom*, Watchtower Bible and Tract Society 1983, p. 188-201

2. *Awake!* December 8 1975, Watchtower Bible and Tract Society,

3. Anthony A. Hokema, *The Four Major Cults*, WM. B. Eerdmans Publishing Co. p. 249

4. Raymond Franz, *In Search of Christian Freedom*, Commentary Press, p. 352-353

5. The Golden Age February 4 1931, Watchtower Bible and Tract Society, p. 293

6. W & J Cetnar, *An Inside View of the Watchtower Society*, published in *Questions for Jehovah's Witnesses*, W.I. Cetnar, p. 64-65

7. *Awake!* August 22 1965, Watchtower Bible and Tract Society, p. 20

8. *Watchtower* November 15 1967, Watchtower Bible and Tract Society, p. 702

9. *Awake!* June 8 1968, Watchtower Bible and Tract Society, p. 21

10. *Watchtower* March 15 1980, Watchtower Bible and Tract Society, p. 31

11. *Jehovah's Witnesses, Proclaimers of God's Kingdom*, Watchtower Bible and Tract Society 1983, p. 199-201

12. J.F. Walvoord & R.B. Zuck, *The Bible Knowledge Commentary*, Scripture Press Publications Inc, p. 719

13. Spiros Zodhiates, *The Complete Word Study Dictionary*, AMG Publishers, p. 1308

14. Robert M. Bowman Jr, *Understanding Jehovah's Witnesses*, Baker Book House, p. 143

15. *Holman Bible Dictionary*, Holman Bible Publishers, p. 320

16. 1 Corinthians 8:2

17. Luke 6:37

18. Anthony A. Hokema, *The Four Major Cults*, WM.

B. Eerdmans Publishing Co. p. 18 & 133

Chapter eight – When things go wrong

1. *Watchtower* September 15 1910, Watchtower Bible and Tract Society, p. 298-299
2. *Watchtower* February 1 1952, Watchtower Bible and Tract Society, p. 79-80
3. *Qualified to be Ministers*, Watchtower Bible and Tract Society, p. 156
4. *Watchtower* February 15 1981, Watchtower Bible and Tract Society, p. 19
5. *Watchtower* January 15 1983, Watchtower Bible and Tract Society, p. 22
6. Raymond Franz, *Crisis of Conscience*, Commentary Press p. 293
7. Quoted in J.A.C. Brown, *Techniques of persuasion*
8. *Jehovah's Witnesses, Proclaimers of God's Kingdom*, Watchtower Bible and Tract Society 1983, p. 187
9. *Watchtower* December 15 1981, Watchtower Bible and Tract Society, p. 27-28
10. *Watchtower* January 1 1983, Watchtower Bible and Tract Society, p. 31
11. *Watchtower* September 15 1981, Watchtower Bible and Tract Society, p. 17
12. *Ibid.*, p. 27
13. *Watchtower* May 15 1985, Watchtower Bible and Tract Society, p.3,4
14. *Organised to Accomplish our ministry*, Watchtower Bible and Tract Society, p.152-153
15. *Watchtower* September 1 1987, Watchtower Bible and Tract Society, p. 13

Chapter nine – A dangerous perspective

1.   Steve Hassan, *Combating Cult Mind Control*, Park Street Press, p. 55, 61, 62, 84

2.   Louise Samways, *Dangerous Persuaders*, Penguin Books, p. 2

3.   *Watchtower* May 1 1984, Watchtower Bible and Tract Society, p. 31

4.   W.C. Stevenson, *Year of Doom, 1975 The inside story of Jehovah's Witnesses*, Hutchinson and Co., p. 108

5.   *Watchtower* July 15 1982, Watchtower Bible and Tract Society, p. 14

6.   *Watchtower* January 15 1983, Watchtower Bible and Tract Society, p. 19-27

7.   Spiros Zodhiates, *The Complete Word Study Dictionary*, AMG Publishers 1992,   p.1018

8.   Spiros Zodhiates, *The Complete Word Study Dictionary*, AMG Publishers 1992,   p.377

9.   *Watchtower* June 15 1989, Watchtower Bible and Tract Society, p. 29

10. *Watchtower* March 1 1989, Watchtower Bible and Tract Society, p. 30

11. *Watchtower* May 15 1990, Watchtower Bible and Tract Society, p. 31

12. *Watchtower* February 15 1990, Watchtower Bible and Tract Society, p. 29

13. Raymond Franz, *Crisis of Conscience*, Commentary Press p. 42

14. M. Scott Peck, *The Road Less Travelled*, Simon and Schuster 1978, p.43,44

Chapter ten – The heart of the matter

1.   Alexander Herzen, *From the Other Shorem, "Omnia*

Mea Mecum Porto", 1855

2. *Jehovah's Witnesses, Proclaimers of God's Kingdom*, Watchtower Bible and Tract Society 1983, p. 676-677

3. Deuteronomy 18:20-22; 13:1-4

4. Raymond Franz, *In Search of Christian Freedom*, Commentary Press, p. 42-50

5. *Watchtower* March 15 1986, Watchtower Bible and Tract Society, p. 20

6. *Watchtower* March 1883, Watchtower Bible and Tract Society, p. 6

7. Anthony A. Hokema, *The Four Major Cults*, WM. B. Eerdmans Publishing Co. p.378

Glossary of Watchtower Society Terms

- Anointed

The 144,000 chosen ones from the book of Revelation chapter 14. These are destined to rule in heaven as Kings and Priests. Not many remain alive today.

- Apostasy

The sin of rejecting the "truth" as defined by the Watchtower Society. Attending a church of a different denomination or subscribing to their beliefs would amount to apostasy.

- Armageddon

The imminent battle between Jehovah God and the forces of the Devil which will result in the annihilation of all those not approved by God.

- Assembly

A larger than normal meeting of Jehovah's Witnesses. Each year one weekend- long "Circuit Assembly" is held for several congregations and one three or four day "District

Assembly" (or Convention) is convened for several Circuits.

- Babylon

A city-state in southern Mesopotamia which took on prominence shortly after 2000 BC. Held to be the source of many false religious doctrines extant today.

- Babylon the Great

The "World empire of false Religion". It includes all of Christendom (except the Witnesses themselves) and all non-Christian religion. Soon to be destroyed immediately before Armageddon.

- Baptism

Total water immersion as a public demonstration that a new Witness has dedicated her life to do God's will as expounded to them by the Watchtower Society.

- Bethel

The name given to the factory, offices, and accommodation of any major branch office of the Witnesses.

- Bible

Inspired word of God. All 66 books are inerrant and inspired. The Old Testament is known to the Witnesses as the Hebrew scriptures and the New Testament as the Greek scriptures.

- Bible study

An arrangement offered for no charge in which a Witness will visit the home of an interested person and conduct a weekly, hour long study using the Watchtower Society's publications. This arrangement is to continue for approximately six months by which stage the student should have demonstrated progress by attending meetings etc.

- Body of Elders

The group of men charged with the spiritual welfare of all within each congregation.

- Book Study

A less formal meeting held in a private home each week using one of the many Watchtower Society' publications as a base.

- Branch Office

The main office of the Watchtower Society in each country.

- Brother

A male baptised member of a congregation. Also the title used to address such a person eg. "Brother Jones."

- Christendom

The most reprehensible part of Babylon the Great. Singled out by the Witnesses for severe criticism due to the "God dishonouring" doctrines it promulgates.

- Christianity

Footstep followers of Jesus Christ. Broken into two sections by the Witnesses: a small group known as "true Christians" (themselves) and a much larger group designated "professed Christians." (Christendom)

- Christ's Return

Held to have taken place invisibly in Heaven in 1914.

- Circuit

A number of congregations (typically 12 or so) organised into a larger group.

- Circuit Overseer

A man charged with the responsibility for the spiritual welfare of all the congregations in his Circuit. He travels continuously, staying with each congregation for one week, receiving accommodation and meals from the local Witnesses.

- Congregation

The basic unit of Jehovah's Witnesses. Usually a geographically convenient pool of Witnesses numbering 50-250.

- Congregation book study

See *Book Study.*

- Creation

The belief that all life was specially created by God in specific periods of time known as "creative days" as described in Genesis.

- Creative days

The days of the Genesis account of creation. Once declared to be 7000 years in duration by the Watchtower Society but now given the less precise length of "millenniums."

- Dates

See individual listings.

- Dedication

The process, prior to baptism, whereby the prospective Witness makes a private dedication to use their life in God's service.

- Disassociation

The act of resigning voluntarily from the Society of Jehovah's Witnesses. A person taking this action is to be treated as a disfellowshiped person.

- Disfellowshiping

A disciplinary action meted out to those who have broken the laws of the Bible or of the Watchtower Society. The disfellowshiped person is evicted from the organisation and remaining Witnesses will have no association with this one.

- District

A number of Circuits organised into a larger group, comprising anywhere from one to two thousand Witnesses.

- District Overseer

A man charged with the spiritual welfare of the Circuits in his District. Also the convenor of the District Assembly.

- Elder

A man appointed to a position of leadership and authority within the congregation. Appointments are from the Branch Office.

- Evolution

The concept that all life arose and then developed by a natural process without intervention from God. Vigorously opposed by the Witnesses.

- Faithful and Discreet slave

See *Anointed.*

- Field Service

The house to house preaching work done by Jehovah's Witnesses throughout the world including return visits and Bible studies.

- Flood

The global deluge recorded in the book of Genesis. Held by the Witnesses to have been an historic event.

- Gentile times

The period of 2,520 years between 607 BC and 1914 AD which is claimed by the Witnesses to represent a period during which God exercised no rule over the earth.

- Goat

From Jesus' parable. One who is opposed to Jehovah's Witnesses.

- God

The Almighty, non-trinitarian and creator of Christ and all things. Personal name Jehovah.

- Governing Body

A small number of Anointed men comprising the chief executive council of the Watchtower Society.

- Great Crowd

The vast majority of Jehovah's Witnesses who hope to live forever in a paradise on earth.

- Group Study

See Book Study

- Har-Magedon

See Armageddon

- Hell

Hades or Sheol. Not a place of torment in Witness theology, merely the resting place of the unconscious dead.

- Holy Spirit

God's impersonal active force. Used by God to accomplish all things. Rendered holy spirit in the New World Translation.

- Inactive

The state of a publisher who has not reported for six months.

- Irregular

The state of a publisher who fails to report during one month in any six month period.

- Jehovah

Personal name of the Almighty. See God and Yahweh.

- Judicial Committee

Special tribunal of Elders convened to investigate suspected or reported wrongdoing on the part of an individual Witness.

- Jesus Christ

Created son of God. Pre-human existence as the Archangel Michael and enthroned in Heaven in 1914. see Christ's return.

- Jews

Once favoured by God as a nation, now only acceptable to Him as individuals.

- Kingdom

The Heavenly government of Jesus Christ and the 144,000 anointed from the earth. Established in 1914 with dominion to extend over the earth in the near future.

- Kingdom Hall

The central meeting place for each congregation. Usually financed and constructed by the Witnesses.

- Last Days

The period of time between Christ's enthronement in 1914 and Armageddon.

- Marking

The process of noting and limiting association with a "disorderly" Witness.

- Memorial

The celebration of Christ's death held annually on the Jewish date of Nisan 14. The emblems of bread and wine are passed with only the anointed partaking. The most important date on the Witness calendar.

- Mind Control

Process of indoctrination used (but not admitted to) by the Witnesses which includes a rejection of independent thinking, conformity to Watchtower Society guidelines, limited association with non-Witnesses, intellectual isolation, and a devolution of decision making.

- Minister

A baptised publisher of Jehovah's Witnesses.

- Ministerial Servant

A man appointed by the Branch Office to care for the more administrative tasks within the congregation such as literature coordinator etc.

- Missionary

A full time minister of Jehovah's Witnesses serving in a foreign assignment.

- Mosaic Law

The law delivered by God to Israel through Moses. Majority not binding on Christians today.

- New System

The anticipated earthly paradise to which most Witnesses look forward. Also known as New Order and New World.

- New World Translation

Version of the Bible translated by a secret committee of Witnesses and first published in the 1950's.

- 1914

The date of Christ's enthronement in Heaven. Also the end of the Gentile times. At one time held to be the date by which Armageddon would arrive.

- 1918

The date scheduled by the Watchtower Society for the destruction of Christendom.

- 1920

All kingdoms of the earth were to be consumed in anarchy by this date.

- 1931

The name "Jehovah's Witnesses" is adopted. This also served to ark a distinction under the new president of the Watchtower Society from the followers of Charles Russell, the former president.

- 1975

End of 6000 years of man's existence on the earth. Widely expected by the Witnesses to mark the end of the Old System.

- Old System

The current world that we live in, ruled by the Devil.

- Organisation

A synonym for the Watchtower Society.

- Other sheep

See Great Crowd.

- Peace and Security

The expected false cry of peace on the earth. Will be followed rapidly by Armageddon.

- Pioneer

A full time minister of Jehovah's Witnesses who agrees to achieve a particular target of hours spent in the field service. Regular pioneers must make 90 hours and special pioneers 140 hours.

- Public Talk

Weekly meeting at which an Elder gives a 45 minute discourse to the congregation from an outline supplied by the Watchtower Society.

- Publisher

A Witness who engages in the field service at least once a month. Weekly participation is the norm.

- Reinstatement

The process by which a disfellowshiped one gains re-entry into the congregation. This usually follows a period of many months where the disfellowshiped person will attend congregation meetings discreetly, usually sitting in the back row without speaking to anyone in attendance.

- Remnant

Those left on earth of the anointed class.

- Report

Monthly statement tendered to the Elders of the amount of time spent and literature sold by each publisher in the field service.

- Resurrection

Act of God in bringing back to life someone dead. The resurrection can be to heavenly life as in the case of the anointed, or to earthly life as for the Great Crowd.

- Return visits

Witnessing work specially concerned with calling back on those who have accepted literature. The aim is for the publisher to start a Bible study.

- Service Meeting

A weekly meeting at the Kingdom Hall designed to encourage field service through talks, demonstrations and audience participation.

- Sheep

From Jesus' parable, Jehovah's Witnesses and potential converts – contrasted with Goats.

- Sister

A female baptised member of a congregation. Also the title used to address such a person eg. "Sister Jones".

- Society

Abbreviation commonly used by Witnesses for Watchtower Bible and Tract Society.

- Soul

The complete person. Not a spiritual entity that may live apart from the individual. The Watchtower Society teaches that man is a soul, not that man has a soul.

- Special Pioneer

A full time publisher who agrees to spend at least 140 hours per month in the field service

- Spirit

1. The breath of life that animates living things. 2. an invisible being including angels and demons.

- Tetragrammaton

Four consonants of the Divine name YHWH. The Latinised form of which is Jehovah.

- Theocratic Ministry School

Weekly school for Witnesses, designed to improve public speaking and teaching skills.

- Trinity

A theological term used to describe God as expressed through the nature of the Father, the Son, and the Holy Spirit. The

Witnesses do not hold to this view but instead view Jesus as God's created son and the Holy Spirit as His impersonal active force

- Truth

A term used by Witnesses to describe the religion to which they belong eg. to be a Witness is to be in the "truth."

- United Nations

Seen in the Witnesses interpretation of Bible prophecy to be the disgusting thing causing desolation and standing where it ought not and the means by which Babylon the Great is destroyed.

- Watchtower

Principle channel through which the Watchtower Society dispenses its teachings. The primary magazine of the Witnesses.

- Watchtower Society

Watchtower Bible and Tract Society. The corporation that is the legal voice of Jehovah's Witnesses and claimed to be spiritually directed by God.

- Watchtower Study

Weekly meeting for Witnesses at which one of the feature articles of the Watchtower magazine is covered in a formalised question and answer fashion with audience participation.

- Witnessing

Work of public preaching or field service.

- Yahweh

Generally preferred rendition (by non-Jehovah's Witnesses) of the tetragrammaton.

- World

Everything outside the Witness community. Any non-approved thinking or conduct would be deemed as "worldly."

Index

1

1914 245
1920 55
1925 55
1931 245
1975 57

6

607 BC 51

A

A framework of values 30
A New World Society 26
Age of the earth 129
An uncomplicated world view 28
Anointed 237, 241, 242
Apostasy 237
Archaeopteryx 126
Armageddon 237
Assemblies and conventions 15, 121, 195, 196, 237, 241

Assembly 237

B

Babylon 46, 47, 50, 77, 238, 239, 249
Babylon the Great 77, 238, 239, 249
Baptism 238
Beliefs of the Witnesses 99
Bethel 238
Bible ... 11, 14, 16, 17, 18, 25, 37, 40, 41, 48, 49, 50, 51, 53, 56, 57, 59, 60, 61, 65, 66, 70, 71, 74, 76, 79, 80, 83, 84, 85, 87, 88, 90, 92, 93, 94, 97, 99, 102, 103, 105, 106, 107, 108, 114, 115, 116, 117, 118, 129, 130, 135, 136, 137, 139, 141, 142, 143, 144, 145, 147, 151, 152, 153, 154, 157, 158, 159, 160, 162, 163, 166, 169, 171, 175, 181, 187, 188, 189, 192, 194, 200, 201, 203, 204, 206, 209, 221, 222, 223, 224, 225, 226, 227, 228, 229, 230, 231, 232, 233, 234, 235, 236, 238, 241, 245, 247, 248, 249
Bible study 14, 19, 187, 188, 189, 238, 247
Birthdays 149, 158, 159, 160, 172
Blood transfusions 77, 103, 149, 152, 153, 154, 155, 158, 172, 175, 194
Body of Elders 239
Book Study 188, 239, 240, 242
Branch Office 239, 241, 244
Brother 90, 96, 239

C

Celebrations 158
Charles Darwin 125
Charles Russell 14, 15, 16, 52, 55, 89, 90, 91, 93, 94, 95, 96
Children 7, 17, 18, 138, 143, 146, 148, 150, 155, 158, 165, 171, 190, 192, 198, 199
Christ 40, 53, 54, 57, 58, 59, 60, 65, 66, 80, 92, 100, 101, 102, 140, 141, 181, 193, 206, 209, 224, 239, 242, 243, 244, 245
Christ's Return 239
Christendom 238, 239, 245

Christianity 55, 101, 203, 206, 207, 239
Christmas 149
Congregation 188, 240
Control 235, 244
Creation 107, 240
Creative days 57, 61, 83, 84, 129, 240
Customs 149

D

Darwinism 123
Devil 73
Disfellowshiping 174, 241
Dress and Grooming 18, 194

E

Easter 149
Eden 61
Education 18, 24, 190
Elder 14, 172, 174, 241, 246
Evolution 124, 128, 230, 231, 241

F

Flood 76, 113, 242
Fossil 120, 126
Franz, Frederick 15, 37
Franz, Raymond 37
Friendships 164

G

Genesis 57, 61, 71, 83, 84, 106, 107, 108, 110, 111, 112, 113, 114,
    115, 116, 119, 129, 144, 145, 146, 152, 153, 158, 200, 226,
    228, 230, 240, 242
Gentile times 242, 245
God's Kingdom ...47, 48, 52, 54, 59, 87, 88, 91, 99, 101, 102, 208,
    221, 222, 223, 224, 225, 226, 227, 228, 229, 232, 233, 234,
    236, 243, 244, 247

Great Crowd 242, 246, 247

I

Identifying the true religion 79
Independent thinking 170, 191, 211, 219, 244
Interference 137, 171, 195, 197
Israelites 51, 137, 138, 139, 140, 142, 143, 153

J

Jehovah 80, 243
Jerusalem 69
Jews 243

L

Last Days 64, 244
Logic 23, 32, 110, 158, 159, 197
Lotteries 149

M

Marking 181, 244
Medicine 152
Military 73, 82, 83, 149
Mistrust of authority 200
Morals 18
Music 18

N

New World Translation ...30, 35, 37, 38, 40, 42, 80, 161, 192, 226, 227, 243, 245
Noah 76, 83, 113, 115, 116, 117, 118, 119, 120, 140, 152, 153, 155, 204

O

Obedience 100, 101, 103, 156, 168, 180, 201, 203, 211
One lord, one faith 76
Organ transplants 156

Organisation 70, 78, 246

P

Peace and Security 68, 246
Pharisees 87, 151, 201
Politics 22, 31, 81, 89, 150, 151
Proof 23, 33, 51, 65, 69, 70
Proof by logic 31
Prophecy...45, 46, 47, 48, 49, 50, 51, 55, 56, 57, 59, 60, 64, 65, 68,
  69, 70, 71, 76, 91, 92, 171, 205, 249
Protection from the world 22

R

Resurrection 102, 247
Rutherford 15, 55, 56, 94, 96, 97, 225

S

Samson 138
Seventh Day Adventists 89, 166, 207
Sexual practices 194
Significant dates ...15, 46, 47, 50, 51, 52, 53, 54, 55, 57, 58, 61, 62,
  63, 64, 65, 66, 67, 68, 70, 101, 156, 189, 210, 233, 235, 239,
  242, 243, 244, 245, 246
Smoking 149, 165

T

The artificial world 186
The creation book 121
The cross 85, 149, 161, 162, 163
The Final Test 73
The garden of Eden 58, 61, 83, 100, 102, 110, 111, 113, 144, 145,
  146, 204
The organisation's founders 90
The Second Coming 53
The second world war 56
The Times of the Nations 46

This Generation 65
Toasting 149
Trade unions 149
Trinity 248
Truth 63, 249

U

United Nations 70, 71, 78, 218, 249

V

Vaccination 155
Voting 148, 150

W

Watchtower magazine... 17, 19, 25, 56, 59, 62, 67, 90, 95, 96, 156,
    170, 188, 189, 190, 198, 200, 249
Watchtower Society... 15, 16, 22, 28, 30, 36, 37, 40, 42, 43, 44, 46,
    48, 51, 52, 53, 54, 57, 58, 59, 60, 61, 62, 63, 65, 67, 70, 71, 76,
    78, 79, 80, 82, 84, 86, 87, 88, 89, 90, 92, 97, 98, 99, 107, 114,
    116, 117, 118, 119, 121, 122, 123, 124, 125, 126, 127, 128,
    129, 130, 131, 132, 133, 134, 135, 139, 141, 145, 147, 151,
    152, 154, 155, 157, 158, 159, 160, 161, 163, 164, 165, 166,
    167, 168, 169, 170, 171, 172, 174, 175, 178, 179, 180, 181,
    182, 184, 185, 186, 187, 188, 189, 190, 191, 192, 193, 195,
    196, 199, 200, 201, 203, 204, 205, 206, 207, 208, 209, 210,
    211, 212, 214, 215, 216, 217, 218, 219, 220, 221, 222, 223,
    224, 225, 226, 227, 228, 229, 230, 231, 232, 233, 234, 235,
    236, 237, 238, 239, 240, 241, 242, 244, 245, 246, 248, 249
Women 138

* 9 7 8 0 9 9 2 2 6 7 5 4 4 *